Children Against Hitler

Children Against
Hitler
The Young Resistance Heroes of the Second World War

By

Monica Porter

PEN & SWORD
HISTORY

AN IMPRINT OF PEN & SWORD BOOKS LTD.
YORKSHIRE – PHILADELPHIA

First published in Great Britain in 2020 and reprinted in 2020 by
Pen & Sword History
An imprint of
Pen & Sword Books Ltd
Yorkshire - Philadelphia

ISBN 978 1 52676 428 7

Printed and bound in the UK by TJ International Ltd, Padstow, Cornwall

Pen & Sword Books Ltd incorporates the Imprints of Pen & Sword Archaeology,
Atlas, Aviation, Battleground, Discovery, Family History, History, Maritime,
Military, Naval, Politics, Railways, Select, Transport, True Crime, Fiction,
Frontline Books, Leo Cooper, Praetorian Press, Seaforth Publishing, Wharncliffe
and White Owl.

For a complete list of Pen & Sword titles please contact

PEN & SWORD BOOKS LIMITED
47 Church Street, Barnsley, South Yorkshire, S70 2AS, England
E-mail: enquiries@pen-and-sword.co.uk
Website: www.pen-and-sword.co.uk

or

PEN AND SWORD BOOKS
1950 Lawrence Rd, Havertown, PA 19083, USA
E-mail: uspen-and-sword@casematepublishers.com
Website: www.penandswordbooks.com

For Dylan, Isaac, Ollie and Ysée

'The young do not know enough to be prudent and therefore they attempt the impossible and achieve it.'

Pearl S. Buck
Winner of the Nobel Prize in Literature, 1938

Contents

Acknowledgements

I am grateful to all those who kindly helped me acquire the photographs for this book and gave permission to use them: Eva Vreeburg of the Image and audiovisual collections of the Noord-Hollands Archief; Filip Bloem, Collection Manager, and Henrik Lundbak, *Museumsinspektør*/Curator, of the Museum of Danish Resistance 1940–1945; Anneke Burger-Tebbens Torringa of the National Hannie Schaft Foundation; Ed Burzminski, son of Stefania and Josef Burzminski; Emanuel Saunders of the Photo Archive of Yad Vashem; Shyla Seller, Archivist of the Vancouver Holocaust Education Centre; Saul Kahn, son of Leon Kahn; Julie Baffet of the Musée de la Résistance Nationale; Claire Lusseyran, daughter of Jacques Lusseyran; Professor Alan Keele of Brigham Young University and BYU's L. Tom Perry Special Collections of the Harold B. Lee Library; Joan Schnibbe, widow of Karl-Heinz Schnibbe; Susanne Brömel of the Gedenkstätte Deutscher Widerstand; Hannah Bayer of Brandes & Apsel Verlag; Ibrahim Basalamah of the NS-Dokumentationszentrum Stadt Köln; Claudia Tamburro and Júlia Balcells Roca of Editions Calmann-Lévy & Editions Kero; Sarah Kaminsky, daughter of Adolfo Kaminsky; Marilyn Duprey of the Mediatheque de Foncine le Haut; Bernard Bouveret; Mark Bles; Stephen Grady and his son, Francis Grady.

My good friend Robin Ashenden – founder and first editor of *Central and Eastern European London Review* – cast his expert editorial eye over the manuscript, which was most useful, as I knew it would be. Professor Helen Fry, eminent historian and author, and happily also a friend, was gracious enough to add her considered views to my closing chapter; a much-appreciated contribution. Anna Swan and John Torode are two respected friends in the print media who have made helpful suggestions. And of course I am thankful for my supportive family. I have dedicated this book to the four grandchildren I am very fortunate to have. I hope that they will one day find in it something of value to their lives.

Lastly I am indebted to all at Pen and Sword Books – a refreshingly human publishing house in an era of impersonal conglomerates – and especially to editors Heather Williams and Gaynor Haliday.

Introduction

Fighting Back

In the prelude to and during the six years of the Second World War, 1939 to 1945, Nazi Germany occupied and held within its grasp, for varying periods, eighteen countries of Europe – as far west as France, as far east as the Soviet Union, north to Norway and south to Greece. It also occupied the British Channel Islands. Many millions of civilians lived with the terror of Nazi domination and they had to make a choice. Would they keep their heads down, stay out of trouble and simply hope to survive until the day of liberation? Or would they collaborate with their occupiers, as this offered immediate protection and would stand them in good stead in the event of a Nazi victory?

There was a third option: resistance. Fighting back, by whatever means possible. This was highly risky. If caught the price to pay was very high: torture, imprisonment in a barbarous concentration camp and, most likely, death. And yet, in every occupied country of Europe, clandestine resistance movements were formed and people risked their lives daily in order to oppose their hated oppressors.

Britain's Special Operations Executive, the legendary SOE, was instrumental from 1941 in organising, supporting and financing this army of the Underground across much of Europe. It trained and parachuted in its own secret agents to work together with local resistance groups, and even developed a special wireless set which resembled an ordinary suitcase, to be used by its operatives for radio communications with SOE headquarters in London. Wartime Prime Minister Winston Churchill instructed the SOE to 'set Europe ablaze!' and it often did.

Resisting took many forms, from the production and dissemination of anti-Nazi newspapers and leaflets, to armed raids against German military and administrative targets. Some resistance members rescued downed Allied pilots and led them to safety in neutral countries, or sheltered Jews evading deportation, others forged documents allowing escapees from Nazi terror to survive with false identities. There were saboteurs who disrupted the fuel supply lines and communication systems so crucial to the German war machine, and spies who enabled Allied intelligence to know in advance the enemy's military plans and take steps to counteract them. Partisan groups camped in the wilds of impenetrable forests waged a damaging guerrilla war against the Germans' traditional armed forces, which were often too slow and unwieldy to react. And there were countless couriers to carry messages, documents, weapons and other prohibited items, and those who smuggled fugitives from one hiding place to another and across borders.

For those with courage and determination, simply standing by and hoping for the war to end was not an option. There was much that could be done meanwhile, and as reward there was the satisfaction of showing the enemy that you could, and would, strike back. But it also meant living in the shadows and being in a constant state of fear, for yourself as well as for your loved ones; the Nazis would make whole families suffer for the actions of a sole member in the resistance. They also retaliated against resistance activities by executing civilians randomly plucked off the streets – and one of the most agonising questions for active fighters of the Underground was whether their bold deeds were worth the sacrifice of others' lives.

So who resisted? Those who believed in a cause greater than themselves. Some were proud patriots who abhorred their country's subjugation by the Nazis. Others held strong Christian beliefs and couldn't stand by and watch the suffering of the persecuted. Communists were of course sworn enemies of the Nazis (although their Soviet-sponsored organisations operated chiefly after Hitler's invasion of the USSR ended the Russo-German non-aggression pact). Still others were Jewish and spurred into action after witnessing the murder of their families and friends. But in truth, anyone who felt a personal compulsion to combat evil was liable to 'go underground'.

They came from all classes and all educational backgrounds – from high school dropouts to scholarly intellectuals – and belonged to virtually all age groups, including children, defined in this book as anyone aged 18 or younger, i.e. of school age, although by the end of the six-year war, if indeed they survived, they would have reached young adulthood. And it's notable how often these youngest of resisters – adolescents with such limited life experience – acted entirely on their own initiative. They weren't ignorant of the risks they were taking. From the very beginning, the administrators of the Third Reich made it abundantly clear to the public how dire were the penalties for opposing them.

Intriguingly, children had a vital advantage over adults in the perilous world of anti-Nazi resistance. Being less cynical, they were more likely to feel invulnerable and to be fearless, to believe they could 'get away with things' no matter how risky their exploits. And that exuded a natural air of self-confidence – often the best defence against detection. Another advantage was the deceptive look of youthful innocence which so often fooled the enemy. They could put on an act, they were streetwise. Of course they might misjudge a person or situation, or fall into a trap. But adults in the Resistance were no less susceptible to such hazards.

Sometimes the parents of adolescent resisters were also involved in their clandestine activities, sometimes they had no knowledge – or only a vague idea – of what their offspring were doing. Often, they didn't want to know the particulars. Loving parents today probably wouldn't countenance the notion of their young children unnecessarily risking their lives for a belief, a principle. But wartime can bring about a great commingling of both personal and communal loyalties, priorities and duties.

Gathered together here are the stories of some of the youngest members of Europe's resistance. All were of school age; the youngest, astonishingly, only 6. They are French, Dutch, Belgian, German, Danish, Polish, Lithuanian, Belorussian, and one is half-French, half-English. They all underwent, in their tender early years, the sorts of horrors which children fortunate enough to be growing up in a time of peace would find difficult to grasp. Through a mixture of resourcefulness, self-belief and good luck, most of these remarkable youngsters outlasted the war and lived to recount their experiences. Some tragically paid for their resistance with their lives. Their tales are a valuable reminder to all generations, and all epochs, that freedom is a precious commodity and not to be taken for granted. It must be cherished and protected and yes, sometimes even fought for.

One wonders what these adolescents from the dark days of the 1930s and 1940s, had they a crystal ball, would have made of their twenty-first century counterparts. Despite the absence of any existential threat – such as that posed for them by Nazi occupation and total war – today's children in a free, democratic Europe, where human rights are respected, seem beset by an epidemic of trauma, unable to cope with the everyday realities of life. According to the World Health Organisation's regional office for Europe, depression and anxiety disorders fall into the top five causes of disease among children and adolescents. More shockingly still, suicide is the leading cause of death for those aged 10 to 19 in the region's low and middle-income countries, and the second-leading cause in high-income countries. What's been going on?

Without doubt much of it can be put down to the malign effects of the age of internet and smartphone addiction: cyberbullying and trolling, the tyranny of social media and especially peer-pressure apps such as Instagram, and sites which openly encourage life-threatening eating disorders, self-harm and suicide. It all adds up to a population of over-digitised children who are largely focused on the self, as epitomised by the ubiquitous 'selfie'. Tech experts themselves have at last begun to recognise the damage inflicted by the likes of Facebook, YouTube and Twitter. In the spring of 2019, former Google engineer Tristan Harris told an audience of Silicon Valley leaders that technology had 'downgraded humanity' by encouraging obsessive and vain behaviour.

There is only one cure for this affliction, as the young heroes in this book would doubtless affirm if they could call out across the great expanse of time: to escape the digital quagmire and find a real cause to believe in. Some of today's children are already achieving this. Perhaps they, along with their intrepid wartime peers, can show the way.

Chapter One

Stefania and Helena Podgorska – The Secret in the Attic

Young Stefania (nicknamed Fusia) was an ordinary country girl, growing up in a village in south-eastern Poland, the daughter of a farmer. Hers was a large family with eight children and like most rural Poles, they were pious Catholics. There was nothing about Fusia that suggested she would perform acts of astonishing courage before she even left her teens, outwitting the adults who turned her world upside down and threatened to destroy her. But two major events occurred which changed the course of her life and transformed it from ordinary to exceptional. Firstly, in 1938, her father fell ill and died. The following year, with her mother's blessing, the 14-year-old Fusia moved to the nearby city of Przemysl, where she got a job at a grocery store owned by the Diamants, a Jewish family. They took to the lively, sweet-natured girl right away. She moved in with them – the elderly Mr and Mrs Diamant and their four grown sons – and they treated her as one of the family.

With Fusia serving behind the counter, more young people came into the store and business picked up. Local lads came in for sweets and cakes, flirted with her and sometimes bought chocolates from the store to give her, which she would usually just put back on the shelves. 'What good business,' Mrs Diamant joked. 'We can sell the same chocolates twice.' Fusia loved the everyday life of the city, much more exciting and fun than being on the farm. So she would sing and dance around the shop. And she enjoyed living in the Diamants' smart apartment and helping Mrs Diamant with the chores.

But then came the second major event, which was a catastrophe for the people of Poland: the invasion in September 1939 by the German army, and the start of the Second World War. Przemysl was the scene of bloody fighting between the German and Polish armies, but as the Poles didn't stand a chance against their mightier enemy they were forced to surrender after only a few days. This defeat was followed by the immediate persecution of the city's Jewish population. Many were killed, while most of the rest were forcibly moved to the eastern half of Przemysl, beyond the River San, which lay in territory now occupied by the Soviet Union as per the Russo-German carve-up of Poland. For a while the Diamants' store stayed open. But supplying it became more difficult. Fusia had to make daily early-morning trips to the main market square to buy foodstuffs to sell to their customers.

The atmosphere on the streets had changed too. Where once Jews and Christians had existed peacefully together, suddenly there was open hostility towards the Jewish people of Przemysl, and Fusia witnessed disturbing episodes of cruelty which she couldn't understand. One day she saw a young Christian boy mistreating a Jewish lad of his own age. Why? There was no apparent difference between them. Her devout mother had taught her that whichever religion people followed, they all prayed to the one God, so you should treat everyone the same.

Then in June 1941 the Peace Pact between the Nazis and the Soviets came to an abrupt end with the German army's attack on the Soviet Union, in the process overrunning and occupying the rest of Poland. The Polish Jews were now doomed. Their businesses were closed down, they were made to wear the humiliating yellow-star badge on their clothes, and before long they were being herded into ghettos.

The Diamants, too, were forced to leave their home and move into the Jewish ghetto in Przemysl, which was sealed off from the rest of the city. Fusia helped them to move in, carrying suitcases and small items of furniture. As a final act of kindness towards their friend and former employee, the Diamants arranged for Fusia to be allowed to remain in one of the rooms of their spacious former apartment. She promised to take care of their home until the family's return. And she managed to get a menial job in a local machine tool factory, to earn enough money to live on.

When she learned that her mother and older brother had been deported to Germany for forced labour and her other siblings were scattered, leaving the youngest – her 6-year-old sister Helena – behind, Fusia took the little girl to live with her in Przemysl. She tried to enlighten Helena, who understood little about the war, as to who the Jews were and why they were being brutally hounded, although Fusia herself didn't really have an answer to that.

For several months, as conditions steadily worsened inside the ghetto – the shortage of food, medicines and fuel, the poor sanitation and increasing incidence of illness – Fusia took many risks in order to help the Diamants, to whom she remained devoted. Non-Jews were not allowed beyond the walls and barbed wire that cut off the ghetto, but by bribing guards and policemen, or simply evading them, she managed to slip in and out, bringing her friends food and clothes and other scarce necessities. Sometimes she crept in by removing the grill on an unguarded basement window.

Being caught would have had grave consequences. She could be imprisoned or deported for slave labour or simply shot there and then. Neither the Nazis nor the Polish policemen who collaborated with them showed much mercy to anyone breaking the rules.

A few times Fusia smuggled out jewellery and other valuables the Diamants had taken into the ghetto, in order to sell them to raise more money for food. She had no idea how to go about this, but eventually tracked down a dodgy 'middleman' who bought the items – for much less than they were worth, of course.

Little Helena gamely played her part too. Reckoning that a small child would be less likely to arouse suspicion, Fusia would give Helena vital messages to carry to the Diamants or one of their Jewish friends, at a pre-arranged time and meeting place along the ghetto boundary. On one such occasion, Helena was about to hand a note through a gate to its recipient when she was spotted by a German guard. 'Hey you!' he shouted at her. 'What are you doing, eh? What have you got there?' Without losing a moment, Helena did what her sister had instructed her to do in case such an event occurred. She crumpled up the note, stuffed it into her mouth, chewed and swallowed it. The angry guard delivered a fierce blow to Helena's face, which knocked her to the ground. As she got up the guard grabbed her. She kicked him hard in the shin, he cried out and as he momentarily let go she darted away.

There had been rumours for a while about planned deportations from the ghetto to the blandly named 'resettlement' camps of Auschwitz, to the west, and Belzec, to the north – fearsome places from which no one ever returned and where, more and more Jews believed, they were being sent to die. The ghetto's inhabitants were desperate to save themselves. But how?

In June 1942 the Diamants' youngest son, Isidore, was carted off, along with a thousand other young men and boys, to the brutal Janowska prison camp outside Lwow, where he was killed. Later that summer the expected deportations by train to the concentration camps began: frightened men, women and children were crammed into cattle cars for the harrowing journey. Along with many of their relatives, Mr and Mrs Diamant (already weakened and frail from their hardships in the ghetto) were amongst the earliest groups to be deported. Two of their remaining sons watched helplessly as guards beat them with rifle butts on the way to the train, and they heard the Germans laughing about how those Jews would be 'made into soap' for the Third Reich.

When Fusia learned about it she was horrified. Could she have done something to save them? Now all she could do was despair.

The 24,000-strong ghetto was slowly diminishing. Fusia saw groups of Jews being marched to the railway station and sometimes shot for failing to obey orders. There were daily scenes of brutality.

Late one cold November night there was a knock on her door. This was an era when the unexpected night-time knock was rarely a good thing, and it alarmed her. Could she have been betrayed to the Nazis' notorious secret police, the Gestapo, for giving clandestine help to her friends in the ghetto? Many Poles were betraying others in return for a financial reward or to gain some other benefit for themselves.

When Fusia opened the door, she did not see menacing Gestapo men in their trademark black leather coats and trilby hats, but a sight that shocked her nevertheless. One of the Diamants' sons, Max, looking dirty, haggard and hounded, with bloodied face and hands, stood there begging to be let inside.

'What has happened to you?' Fusia pulled him into the room and he collapsed in a chair. By now Helena was awake and staring at their bloodied visitor, afraid and confused. Fusia brought warm water to clean Max's face and hands, and together the two sisters tended to the son of Fusia's former employers. Meanwhile he recounted his story of the past two days.

'They came for us in the ghetto and beat us with sticks, then put us on the train to Belzec – me, my brother Chaim and our two cousins. We were packed tightly into the cattle wagons, not enough room to sit down. People were suffocating. But I refused to be taken to my death. I had already made up my mind to jump from the moving train, and had brought a pair of pliers with me. I managed to be near one of the narrow windows covered with barbed wire. I cut it away. If I died in the escape, that was better than what the Nazis had in store for us. I beseeched Chaim and our cousins to jump out after me. But they wouldn't. Now I'm afraid I will never see them again.'

Max said that when he hit the ground he was knocked unconscious for a while. After he came to, cut and bruised, he hid in the nearby forest, waiting until dark before making his slow and painful way back through the countryside to Przemysl. Hoping that Fusia would still be living in her room at the family's old apartment, he took the risk and knocked on the door. He had nowhere else to go. Could he stay the night?

'Of course.' Fusia gave Max her bed and said she would share Helena's bed with her. 'I'm sorry I have no pyjamas for you, but you can wear my nightgown.'

The nightgown looked comical on Max and Helena started giggling. 'Now there are two Fusias,' she said. Max managed a weak smile.

But he was inconsolable, for he had lost everything and everyone. All night long he called out feverishly for his parents and for the brother who hadn't followed him off the train. 'Chaim! Why didn't you jump?' Fusia sat by his bed, trying to calm him, afraid someone might hear him and wonder about the strange man staying in the room of two young sisters.

In the morning she made Max some tea and he felt a little better. Fusia told him he could remain with her but he must never leave the room, and should any visitor come to the door, he would have to hide under the bed, together with all his belongings, and be absolutely still. 'Don't breathe too loudly. Don't sneeze. And don't let your feet stick out!'

To Helena she said: 'You must never, ever tell anyone about Max. Not your friends, not the neighbours. Do you understand? This has to be our secret. Or the very bad people in our country will kill us all.' And so began the Podgorska sisters' two years of defying the Nazis by sheltering Jews.

Max now approached Fusia tentatively, to ask whether she could also help rescue his younger brother Henek and his fiancée Danuta, the only family he had left. They were still in the ghetto but during the day were taken with other Jews as part of a work detail to toil on a farm outside the city. Fusia agreed. One day she went to the field where they were working. Out of earshot of the guards, she managed to tell them that Max was alive and staying with her, and that they also had to flee from the ghetto before it was too late.

Danuta, who had long feared the worst, was eager to escape: 'I know that once they have no further use for us we will be killed.' But Henek was reluctant. It would take another few weeks before he agreed to flee the ghetto with Danuta and join Max in hiding. But of course all three of them couldn't stay in the sisters' single room and hide under the bed when someone came to the door. Fusia would have to find larger accommodation, urgently. And somehow to afford the rent.

She had an idea. There was a pleasant young woman called Maria living in her apartment building with whom Fusia had become friends. She decided to approach her.

'Listen Maria,' she began, 'they are killing Jews and taking them away to concentration camps. Perhaps we can do something for them. Together we can find a bigger apartment and a few of my Jewish friends can come there, and you can take in a few – you have Jewish friends, don't you? – and that way we can help them.'

Maria gave her friend a clear, conclusive answer. 'Fusia, I am 21. You are 17. You saw the posters the Gestapo have put up on the streets, the ones saying "The punishment for anyone caught helping Jews is death". I'm too young to go to the grave for a Jew. But if you want to risk dying at your age, that's your choice.'

Now Fusia was anxious. It would be very dangerous for her if Maria were unthinkingly to repeat her proposal. Could she be trusted to keep quiet? 'All right,' she said. 'I understand. But please don't mention to anybody that I suggested this to you.'

Maria grinned. 'Don't worry. I've already got amnesia.'

Obviously, Fusia would have to find a bigger place on her own. But accommodation was in short supply. The city was full of uninhabitable bombed houses, often missing their doors, floorboards and windows, as people salvaged wood for fuel. As she searched the city she grew ever more desperate. Standing in the street one day, not knowing which way to turn, the devout young Christian drew upon her faith and prayed for guidance. A moment later she noticed two street cleaners nearby, middle-aged women idly leaning on their brooms, chatting. A sixth sense told her they could help. She walked over to them, smiling apologetically.

'Excuse me, ladies. I've been looking for a place to live, for me and my little sister, but can't find anything. Are you familiar with this area? Do you perhaps know of an available apartment somewhere?'

The two women exchanged glances. 'As it happens,' replied one of them, 'I do know of a place which might suit you. It's just been vacated, so no one yet knows about it.' She added proudly: 'I'm friendly with the caretaker there.'

And that was how Fusia found the little cottage on Tatarska Street, on the outskirts of the city. There was no electricity or running water and only an outdoor toilet. But it had two rooms and a kitchen, plus – and this was the crucial factor – a large attic. Attics were very good for concealing people.

Fusia and Helena moved in first. And over the course of the following weeks came Max, Henek and Danuta, as well as four others from the ghetto whom Fusia had agreed to take in on the basis that

'If they shoot me for hiding three Jews they might as well shoot me for seven'. They were Henek's friends Wilhelm Schillinger and his young daughter Krystyna, Siunek Hirsch and his elderly father Leon.

Escaping from the ghetto disguised as ordinary Poles, wearing workmen's clothes, Wilhelm and Siunek were lucky not to be stopped along the way by police or soldiers and asked for identity papers, which they didn't possess. Leon Hirsch did, however, have a heart-stopping moment. Nearing Tatarska Street he was grabbed by a stranger and pulled inside a house. 'I know you're a Jew and you are going to hide with some Polish family around here. I need money. You Jews are rich. Give me your money.' Terrified, Hirsch gave him all the money he had with him, then pleaded: 'Please, may I go now?' The Pole looked out of his doorway and said 'Wait. There are policemen on the street. I'll tell you when it's safe.' And after a while: 'Okay, they have moved off, so go now, quickly.' And he added: 'I may be a thief but I'm not a murderer. Good luck. Maybe we'll meet again after the war.'

The men's first task at the cottage was to construct a false wall in the attic, creating a secret space in which the fugitives could conceal themselves should any outsider find reason to climb the ladder and look into the attic. The wall must appear to be an original part of the cottage, old and weathered and of the same type of wood, in order to avoid suspicion.

After an exhaustive search, Fusia found a man at the market selling old boards and planks from ruined homes, and bought a large pile, telling him – and the nosy new neighbours who saw it being delivered to her door – that she needed it for firewood for the winter.

Two metres were divided off from the length of the attic and the life-saving wall was nailed into place. The secret compartment behind it was nicknamed the 'bunker'.

Not long after the seven escapees had settled into their new attic home, two teenaged boys came to the cottage with a letter for Fusia. They told her it was from a woman in the ghetto, who was paying them to deliver it. They needed her signature as proof of delivery.

As Fusia read the handwritten letter from a woman she didn't know called Mrs Zimmerman, she became flushed with anger. She was fearful too. 'I know that you are hiding Jews,' wrote the woman, who proceeded to name some of people Fusia was sheltering. 'You must also accept my two children and me. If you don't, I will denounce you to the Gestapo.' She told Fusia to come to the ghetto to make the necessary arrangements with her.

Setting down on paper these incriminating words and then entrusting them to two unknown 'street boys' was life-endangering – for her and Helena and for the seven in the attic – and Fusia was furious with this Zimmerman woman, whoever she was. After dark, she slipped into the ghetto to find her and eventually located a woman so desperate to save her children that she was prepared to do anything. Still, the letter was inexcusable. 'How dare you blackmail me like this and risk everyone's life? You didn't have to do that!'

Mrs Zimmerman fell to her knees, cried and kissed Fusia's hands, begging to be forgiven. 'Please, it was the only thing I could think of. I know it was wrong, But I don't want my children to die.' She had a son aged 8 and a daughter of 14. As Fusia gazed at the frightened, tearful youngsters cowering together in a corner, she softened. In the end she consented to taking the three of them. Mrs Zimmerman embraced her, murmuring numerous 'thank yous' and kissing her hands again.

There would now be a crowd of ten in the attic: a lot of mouths to feed in secret at a little cottage supposedly home to only two girls.

As the summer of 1943 wore on, the Nazis' liquidation of the Przemysl ghetto was nearly complete. When at last the final *aktion* (as the Germans termed the round-up and deportation of a trainload of Jews) took place, the attic received its final three refugees.

Apparently Leon Hirsch had made a promise to relatives – his newly married young nephew Munio and his wife Stefania, plus his cousin Janek – that they could join him in hiding, and felt honour-bound to fulfil it. As he had done this without Fusia's knowledge, she was once again angry at having her arm twisted, and at the increased danger. But when, after a nerve-racking walk through the city, dodging police searches, the three arrived and beseeched Fusia not to throw them out because they would all be killed, she gave a hopeless sigh and ushered them in. And that made thirteen.

To supplement Fusia's modest income from her factory job, she and some of the women in the attic began knitting sweaters, scarves and hats from scraps of old clothes and fabrics bought in the market. They were then re-sold in the market or to neighbours. Soon she was taking orders for sweaters from friends and acquaintances. With the extra money she earned she bought food for the hidden thirteen, travelling out to farms for vegetables when the shops ran short. So as not to arouse suspicion about the large quantities of bread and potatoes she and Helena were seen carrying home, they pretended to be buying and selling them on the black market (a common practice in those grim days).

Now 8 years old, Helena busied herself washing the fugitives' clothes, bringing them food and water and removing refuse from the attic. She was as keenly aware as her older sister that should they be discovered harbouring Jews they would be killed, no questions asked. Yet she never showed fear or reluctance to help. She devoted herself calmly to the mission at hand with a child's blind faith that all would be well, which was a fortunate trait as it doubtless helped to deflect unwanted attention from curious and potentially ill-intentioned locals. She looked like any ordinary little Polish girl, just trying, despite all the deprivations, to get through the war.

For Fusia there was an added complication: boys. The attractive teenager was naturally asked out on dates, and one boy in particular was very drawn to her. She returned his affections. But how could she have a suitor? It was impossible. She couldn't invite someone home for the evening with thirteen clandestine occupants above their heads. So whenever he asked her out, she simply told him: 'Let's wait till after the war. It makes no sense being together now. We don't know what will happen. We can be killed any day.'

But he was persistent. 'I love you, Fusia. I want us to get married.'

She tried not to show her true feelings for this decent, nice-looking boy. If it weren't for her secret 'mission' she would gladly have been with him. 'I'm sorry, we can't.'

Sometimes he walked her home from work, always asking to come in. Her strict Catholic upbringing offered a reasonable argument:

'No, my sister is here and I must set a good example. I can't bring a boy home, it isn't right. And the neighbours will talk.'

What if he began to suspect her? What if he thought she was hiding something? Despite his claim that he loved her, she knew she couldn't confide in him. It was too risky. No, she would have to end this little liaison for good. She thought of a solution. A friend of hers had a photographic studio where a few of the German soldiers, including the most brutal of them – the SS – went to have their pictures taken. They would then proudly send these photos to their families or girlfriends back home: *Here I am in Poland, fighting for the Fatherland. Heil Hitler!* One morning Fusia stopped by the studio to ask a favour of her friend. 'Have you taken any pictures lately of young German soldiers?' Her friend said that in fact she had, only the day before, and she produced a photo of a handsome young soldier in SS uniform, awaiting collection. 'That's perfect!' Fusia exclaimed. 'Could you make a copy and frame it for me?'

'All right. But what on earth for?'

'Please just do it.'

Her friend told her to come back for it the next day.

The next time Fusia's eager suitor walked her home from work, she allowed him to escort her inside. As he entered the main room of the cottage, which was also her bedroom, he immediately noticed the framed photo of the SS soldier hanging on the wall above her bed. He stared at it for a moment.

'What's this?' he asked.

'That's my boyfriend,' Fusia answered quietly.

He looked at her in disbelief. '*You*, Fusia? You are going with a Nazi?'

She nodded, then looked away.

His expression turned from incredulity to hurt, to disgust. Polish girls who went with men of the occupying Nazi forces were considered traitors and scorned. 'I will never forgive you,' he said, his voice trembling with emotion. Then he turned around and left.

Fusia had an urge to run after him, embrace him and explain everything. Of course she was no traitor, had no Nazi boyfriend!

But instead she stood by the window and watched, heartbroken, as he walked away.

He never spoke to her again.

It wasn't easy for thirteen people, especially as three of them were children, to remain quiet day and night, to stay cooped up indoors, to talk in whispers and keep a constant vigil through small holes in the attic wall in case the authorities should unexpectedly turn up outside. They were always apprehensive. But somehow they carried on. As for Fusia, she struggled to keep them all fed and looked after. Each morning she went off to the factory, where every so often, to her alarm, the Gestapo would arrive. They would question the workers and often take a 'suspect' person away. Those people never returned. Whenever the Gestapo came Fusia tensed up, her heart pounding. *Are they coming for me this time?* And at the end of every day as she made her way home, she wondered what she would find when she got there. Was everyone still safe? Or had they been betrayed, taken away, never to be seen again? Perhaps the Gestapo was waiting there for her, in order to bundle her into a car and take her off to some terrible end.

But the most dangerous moment happened in quite a different manner, one day in early 1944, with the sudden appearance of two brusque SS men at the cottage door. They coldly informed Fusia that the German army was taking over the school across the road for use as a field hospital and they required living quarters for its medical personnel.

'How many rooms have you here?' they demanded, looking around the property.

'Two.'

'And how many live here?'

'My sister and I.'

'Two girls don't need so much space. This house will be requisitioned by the German Reich. You have two hours to pack your things and leave. If you are still here when we return, you will both be shot.'

A desperate Fusia ran out to begin a frantic search of the neigh-bourhood for alternative accommodation: someplace big enough for thirteen secret residents. But it was a hopeless task. All liveable quarters were already occupied, leaving only derelict buildings. And even if some suitable new place should be available, how could she possibly smuggle that large group out of the attic and out through the streets – all within two hours? She returned home in despair.

'Save yourself and Helena,' Max urged her. 'Go now and leave us here. You have done so much for us, but we are finished. There is nothing more you can do. Don't die with us.'

Fusia refused to go. She couldn't bring herself to abandon the people in her care. But time was running out and the two-hour deadline was almost up. As always when she didn't know what to do, the staunch Catholic got down on her knees and prayed. The others gathered around and knelt beside her, murmuring prayers of their own but, as Fusia's mother had said, 'to the same God'.

A few minutes later she stood up. 'It's going to be all right,' she reassured everyone, with clear-eyed confidence. 'Go up to the bunker and be very quiet. The SS will be back very soon. But don't worry, I am not leaving. And you will be safe there.'

The Jews stared at the girl as if she had lost her mind. How could she be so sure of this? But they did as she asked. Meanwhile Fusia threw open the window and to everyone's astonishment began to clean and tidy the cottage, singing cheerfully.

A little later an SS man arrived at the door – a different one this time. He laughed as he heard Fusia's carefree singing. 'Ah, Fraulein, I see you are still here,' he said in broken Polish. 'That's fine. It turns out we need only one of your rooms. We will take the room at the rear for two of our nurses. You and your sister can remain here in this one.' And still smiling, he strode off.

To Fusia, this abrupt reversal of fortune was proof that her prayer had been answered. God had worked a miracle. But whether a miracle or merely an astounding stroke of good luck, once again they had made it through. Ten minutes later two young German nurses in uniform entered briskly, carrying their baggage. With curt nods at Fusia they settled into the room at the back, situated directly beneath the bunker, and began chatting to each other.

This created a whole new level of peril. The thirteen secret residents, fugitives from the Nazis, would now have to remain undetected with the enemy living in the same house, a few feet below them. Surely it would prove an impossible challenge.

During the day the nurses were out, working at the field hospital. But each evening they arrived back and soon afterwards their boy-friends, Wehrmacht soldiers, would come to visit them. Fusia always shuddered when they turned up, rifles slung over their shoulders. Armed Nazis guests in her home! At times the tension was excruciating. The nurses would cook supper for themselves and their boyfriends in the kitchen, with the tantalising aromas of sizzling meat and hearty soups drifting upwards to torment the fugitives who subsisted on a diet mainly of bread and potatoes. After dinner, the Nazi foursome would sing and laugh and canoodle the night away.

Early on in their occupancy, dissatisfied with the kerosene lamps and candles, the Germans decided to install electricity. Two soldiers arrived with the necessary equipment and announced that they were going to run a cable through the roof. To Fusia's horror, they began to make a hole directly over the heads of the fugitives.

'Oh no, please! You can't do that!' she cried.

'Why not?'

'Well … with a hole in the roof, the rain will come in. Surely you can run the cable through the window downstairs?'

After a moment one soldier turned to the other and said, 'You know, she's right.'

Another close call.

Even though the Jews hardly dared breathe at night with the German lodgers below, it was impossible for thirteen people to be absolutely still and quiet. A muffled cough (it was winter, after all, and the attic was unheated), the squeak of a floorboard, a rustle of clothes or bedding in the cramped quarters – any unexpected sound might give them away.

And then it happened. Late one night one of the nurses heard a noise above her head which aroused her suspicion. The next day, as Fusia arrived home from work, she found the nurses and their boyfriends there, together with an unknown SS man. One of the nurses grabbed her by the arm and started questioning her about the attic, while the other started up the ladder, certain that something fishy was going on up there. Fusia wanted to run after her but she was held back. The thought flashed into her mind: is this how it ends?

The suspicious nurse opened the hatch, peered into the attic and looked around. But she saw only the unwanted broken furniture, dusty trunks and piles of old clothes that Fusia had deliberately put there to make it look like an ordinary attic used for storing junk.

'Ugh,' she said, coming back down. 'It's so dirty up there.' But she signalled to the others that everything was in order.

On this occasion the Jews owed their salvation to Max. Having heard the noisy arrival of the five Germans and fearing that they must suspect something, as a precaution he hurriedly ushered everyone into the bunker. Behind the false wall they were as invisible as ghosts and the Germans concluded that the mysterious sound the nurse had heard was most likely made by rats.

The months passed. As winter turned to spring, the Russians approached from the east and the Nazis retreated westward. The Front grew ever closer and by midsummer, fighting could be heard in the distance. When the Red Army reached the outskirts of Przemysl, the field hospital was hastily evacuated. Fusia's nurses packed their bags and fled along with the rest of the medical staff.

For days the battle raged in and around the city. Fusia and Helena didn't dare go outdoors, not even to search for food, although they had almost nothing left to eat. The frightening bombardment from mortar shells, the machine-gun and rifle fire went on all night long – until one morning it all stopped. And suddenly it was eerily quiet in the city.

Could it be that their long nightmare was over at last? Ever cautious, Fusia told her Jews to remain in the bunker while she tried to find out what was happening. She opened her window, leaned out and observed the goings-on in the street.

Two Russian soldiers were passing by. They noticed saw her, stopped and approached the window. Fusia spoke a little Russian.

The soldiers indicated that they wanted to come in, she said yes, and once inside they asked whether she had any vodka. She poured them what little vodka she had left. They wanted to know who lived at the cottage.

'Just me and my sister.' Helena was standing beside her, gazing up at the first Russian soldiers she had ever seen, wondering what their arrival would mean for them.

'Will the Germans be back?' asked Fusia.

'Oh no!' came their hearty reply. 'We have pushed them far away from here. They won't be back.'

The fugitives, who had been listening to the conversation from above, now hurried down the ladder, overjoyed at what they heard.

Startled by the abrupt appearance of the motley group, the soldiers raised their rifles, demanding to know who they were. Fusia pleaded with them to lower their weapons, explaining that they were Jews whom she and Helena had been sheltering from the Nazis, for a little over two years.

'Jews?' said one of Russians in amazement. 'I am a Jew.'

And the thirteen 'ghosts', pale and thin and barely able to walk after their long confinement, wept with relief and kissed the soldiers who in turn gazed at Fusia and Helena and marvelled: 'So many Jews, saved by these two girls! Not even two girls, but a girl and half!' They laughed and hailed the sisters as *geroi* – heroes. The attic had kept its secret. They had all survived and their private war was over. The fact that the two sisters had carried out their lengthy, death-defying rescue mission entirely alone, without the assistance, encouragement or even the knowledge of any organised resistance group, is almost inconceivable.

Chapter Two

Leibke Kaganowicz – The Fighter in the Forest

There is an old perception that the Jewish populations of Europe went meekly to their deaths during the Second World War, that they were led by the Nazis and their collaborators, as the Biblical phrase goes, 'like lambs to the slaughter'. And it is true that the vast majority of the annihilated did not rebel when ordered on to cattle trains bound for the death camps or marched to one of the many other sites of mass execution.

Why not? For one thing, very few could have imagined the horror that lay ahead of them. Who would have believed that a sophisticated, highly cultured nation such as Germany was capable of committing such barbarities? And it is human nature to be hopeful, to dispel one's worst fears and have faith that somehow things will be all right; despite signs and warnings to the contrary.

But some Jews did refuse to be led, to give their self-appointed masters the benefit of the doubt. They resisted, ran away, and when they had gathered their strength they fought back, hard. They became partisans, members of organised groups of armed resistance fighters. Partisans belonged to various categories. Some operated under the auspices of the Soviet Union and were highly politicised communists. Others were proud patriots, be they Poles, Ukrainians, Frenchmen and so forth. These two categories didn't always get along; they mistrusted each other. They had a common enemy, but while the patriots aimed to reinstate national sovereignty and democracy after the defeat of Nazi Germany, the communists were widely suspected (and with justification) of planning instead for a communist state under the sponsorship of Stalin's Russia.

And then there were the Jewish partisans, mostly escapees from the ghettos, some of whom later became famous (for example the Bielski brothers from Belorussia, portrayed in the 2008 film *Defiance*, starring Daniel Craig). An estimated 25,000 Jewish partisans were active in Nazi-occupied Europe. Many perished during the war but others survived and as well as battling Hitler's war machine, these fighters saved the lives of a significant number of their fellow Jews: men, women and children.

One of the youngest Jewish partisans was 16-year-old Leibke Kaganowicz. He was born in the small town of Eisiskes in south-eastern Lithuania. His father was a local merchant (well liked if not particularly successful), he had a kind and loving mother, and he was close to his older brother Benjamin and younger sister Frieda. They had a humble lifestyle but his childhood within their traditional, close-knit Jewish community was a happy one ... until June 1941, when the Nazis invaded and the long nightmare began.

The persecution of the town's mostly Jewish population, some 3,500 souls, started at once. It was the same story as almost everywhere else in Nazi-occupied Europe: neighbours, friends, colleagues with whom the Jews had formerly co-existed in harmony suddenly became their enemies, tormenting and attacking them and looting their homes. Rumours circulated about truckloads of Jews being taken away from neighbouring towns and villages to an unknown fate. Some said they were being killed. Everyone was nervous. But they told themselves it simply couldn't be true. After all, Jews had been living in Eisiskes for more than 900 years and had endured some hard times. Surely they could survive this calamity too.

But in late September, at last, the Nazis launched their programme of annihilation of the town's Jews with a mass round-up. Leibke and his brother Benjamin, refusing to be herded with the others, went into hiding in the town. Unavoidably separated from their parents and sister, they had no idea of their fate.

After a few days of desperately dodging murderous Lithuanian policemen and gendarmes, with many close calls, and weak from hunger and lack of sleep, the two boys decided to find a better temporary hiding place, under cover of darkness. They remembered the old, overgrown Catholic cemetery a little way out of town, beside a gravel pit. They had played there as children and knew it well. There they would be safe. They made their way to the cemetery and found a spot beneath tangled bushes alongside the boundary wall, where they slept for a few hours.

In the morning they were awakened by the terrifying sounds of people screaming, shouting, crying. And then Leibke witnessed a horrifying sight which he would never forget, but which would give him the strength and resolve – the rage he needed – to fight back. The women and children of Eisiskes were being whipped and hurried along the road in large groups by the Nazis' Lithuanian collaborators, towards the gravel pit. There they were made to strip before being marched to the edge of the pit and shot. Peering over the cemetery wall, Leibke and Benjamin watched as those they had grown up with and cared for were brutally wiped out, including their aunt and their beloved cousin Sarah, 'the most beautiful girl in town'.

Leibke wanted to scream in revulsion and run away, to make it all end, but somehow he couldn't stop watching. It was as if he had to commit to memory each fragment of this unimaginable crime and the face of every murderer.

'Don't look, Leibke! Don't look!' Benjamin sobbed, pulling his brother away, begging him to lie down beside him.

But Leibke wouldn't lie down. He forced himself to keep looking until the last group had been dispatched into the pit, the murderers had left and it was quiet again.

At nightfall, Leibke and Benjamin fled. For weeks they were on the run, begging food from the few local farmers they dared to trust, sleeping in barns, never staying anywhere for more than a day or two. During this time they were overjoyed to learn that, miraculously, the rest of their family had evaded the massacre and were safe, in hiding.

Reunited, they decided to travel together to Radun, a larger town a few hours away, where they had relatives. There the Jews were still living in their ghetto and getting on with their lives. They were hard workers with useful skills and trades. Perhaps, the Jews reasoned, the Nazis would therefore spare them. Perhaps the killings were over now.

Their relatives welcomed them warmly, took them in and for a while things carried on more or less calmly. But in the spring there were signs that the Jews of Radun would soon meet the same fate as those in Eisiskes. Then the *Einsatzgruppen* – Nazi death squads – turned up and the executions commenced.

Hiding in an attic, the Kaganowicz family managed once more, by great good fortune, to survive the slaughter. And this time Leibke vowed never again to be imprisoned in a ghetto. He had heard of the partisans, living on their own terms, surviving in their encampments in the region's great, dense forests – impenetrable to most people – and emerging to perform daring sabotage missions. Striking back at the enemy, guerrilla-style, wherever and however they could. Avenging their dead. And he desperately wanted to join them.

But Leibke needed to convince his reluctant father to let him go. 'I have to do it, Papa,' he argued. 'I can't wait around to be killed. I must learn to fight. And there are family groups in the forest too, living just as the partisans do. It isn't an easy life, it's primitive, but it's our family's only chance to be safe. At least we'll be able to sleep at night and get enough food so that our stomachs aren't growling all the time.'

And so it was decided. Leibke, his siblings and their father would make contact with the partisans and head for the forest. His mother alone refused to go. 'Your grandmother could never survive in the forest, she can't adjust to that kind of life at her age. And I won't leave her behind. I must stay and take care of her. You go and save yourselves.'

They begged her to change her mind but she was adamant. With great sadness, they bid her goodbye. They would never see her again.

For the rest of his life Leibke would be haunted by the memory of that reluctant parting from his mother, racked with guilt that he hadn't somehow persuaded her to come with them.

They bought two rifles from a sympathetic farmer, then trekked for several days to another farm, whose owner lived on the edge of the ancient forest and was a contact man for the partisans and the families living deep inside it. Throughout the night he guided Leibke and his family towards their sanctuary, crossing swamps, through dense thickets and kilometres of heavy forest.

When they arrived at the family camp just after dawn, they were met with the heartening sight of some hundred-odd Jewish people living openly and apparently without fear. There were children laughing and playing, women cooking breakfast over open fires, men shaving and washing themselves with buckets of water. They were greeted by friends who helped them construct a wooden shelter and make mattresses of evergreen branches. For the first time in a year they could relax a little. The camp covered 50 acres of high ground, in the middle of a swamp which could be crossed only by stepping on partly submerged logs. It was an ingenious hidden refuge. Of course there were armed sentries posted in the forest, keeping any eye out for any unexpected intruders. And for added protection, the partisans' camp was only a kilometre or so away.

Leibke left his family in the haven of the family camp and joined the partisans, a group of about thirty able-bodied young Russians and Jews. 'This is what I have been waiting for,' he told them, 'a chance to be a hunter instead of one of the hunted.'

Nicknaming him *patsan*, the Russian word for 'little kid', Leibke was taught to use arms to defend himself. He learnt how to handle a rifle, machine gun and grenade, as well as how to set dynamite to blow up trains, bridges and buildings. This was the art of guerrilla warfare: hit-and-run raids by small teams, designed for maximum damage to your enemy at minimum cost to you. He and his comrades cut down power lines and telephone poles. They derailed trains by unscrewing the rails, then heating them up with fire and once they were sufficiently pliable, curling them around a tree. The key aim of the partisans was sabotage: disrupting the Nazis' war effort by ruining their lines of communication and interrupting their transportation of troops and essential supplies, especially of fuel.

In time, after joining a larger partisan brigade, Leibke became a specialist in blowing up trains. He and his small sabotage unit were given mines which consisted of 20lbs of pressed dynamite, wrapped in burlap and tied with rope, which had to be laid in between the ties under the rails. Then, hiding a short distance away, they would wait for the train to come rumbling down the line. The shock wave from the explosion sometimes knocked them flat on their backs. But the excitement at seeing the smashed and flaming derailed wreckage and the satisfaction of having struck a blow for their cause were almost overwhelming.

It was dangerous work, of course. Not only because the railways were heavily guarded by soldiers and saboteurs could easily be spotted and killed, but because the mines were volatile and had to be handled with great care. They had to be prepared and laid quickly and efficiently – always in the dark of night – and well timed to coincide with the train's approach.

Eventually they received a supply of English magnetic mines, designed to be attached to the trains themselves – under the very noses of patrolling guards. Containing a timing mechanism, these mines could be set to explode hours later. By the time the explosion came the train might be hundreds of kilometres away at the Front, where it would do the most damage.

There were a few dicey occasions when different sabotage units, unexpectedly encountering each other in the dark and mistaking each other for the enemy, would exchange fire. But in time they all became better organised and carved out their own territories for carrying out missions.

On one occasion, as they prepared for a rare daylight mission, Leibke played a practical joke on a member of his unit, a young man called Michka. He and fellow saboteur Cymbal had agreed to meet Michka (who would be bringing along the mine) by a certain bridge. As Leibke and Cymbal waited for him, they saw him approaching from the far side of a field. Leibke grabbed Cymbal's arm and pulled him behind some bushes. As Michka came near, Leibke shouted in German: 'Halt, you cursed Jew!'

A terrified Michka spun around and fled, heading so fast through the scrub and into the forest that he didn't hear Leibke call after him: 'Stop, Michka, it's only me!'

But he wasn't stopping for anyone. Leibke and Cymbal chased after him but couldn't catch up. At last they set off for the location of their mission, hoping to rendezvous with Michka there. It was evening when their exhausted comrade finally turned up, his clothes muddied and torn. Leibke and Cymbal burst out laughing.

'What's so funny?' Michka demanded.

'I heard you were chased by Germans,' Leibke replied.

'How do you know?'

'Halt, you cursed Jew!' said Leibke, in the same gruff German voice as before.

Michka exploded with rage and in an instant was aiming his rifle at the prankster. Cymbal wrestled him to the ground and took the weapon away. After things had calmed down, Leibke apologised and admitted he'd been a fool.

Now they realised they had a far greater problem to worry about. In his fright at being captured by Germans, Michka had dropped the mine somewhere in the undergrowth. For a partisan to lose his explosives meant death by firing squad, a punishment intended to deter carelessness and the squandering of essential resources. All explosives had to be accounted for. They had no choice but to find the missing mine, wherever it was, and carry out their planned mission.

All the next day, as long as there was daylight, they looked for it but it was nowhere to be found. Then, through a lucky twist of fate, they saw how they might be saved from the firing squad. As darkness fell another partisan unit moved into their area, set a mine and blew up a train. If only they could somehow take the credit for this successful operation, they could return to their partisan leaders without fear and claim mission accomplished.

They quickly set off in search of the liaison man for local partisan activity, with the idea of persuading him to give them credit for the other unit's explosion. A long shot, but probably their only hope.

They found the liaison man. But even before they could speak he greeted them with: 'A great piece of work, boys! Congratulations on your triumph.' Leibke and the others graciously accepted the praise and, much relieved, hurried on their way.

By 1943 there were more than 100,000 partisan fighters, men and women, operating in Leibke's area – the towns and villages of the borderlands of Lithuania, Poland and Belorussia – and encamped in its primeval forests. One of their biggest concerns was securing enough food for them all. Sometimes groups would requisition food from local farmers. But the Germans themselves ended up inadvertently providing much of it, to their fury. They had set up depots to which farmers were forced to deliver their produce, intended to feed Wehrmacht troops fighting on the Eastern Front. These depots were guarded by the gendarmerie but regularly attacked and raided by partisans.

On May Day, the major holiday in the Soviet Union to celebrate workers, Leibke took part in an attack on such a depot. It was filled with big crates of butter, cheese and eggs, all packed in straw. After overcoming the hapless gendarmes they took all they could carry and destroyed the rest. Leibke joyfully stomped all over the trays of eggs, smashing them by the thousands, relishing the fact that they would not go towards sustaining the enemy. On their return to the forest they enjoyed a magnificent May Day feast.

On the whole though their diet was poor, and together with a lack of bathing facilities, that led to all sorts of health problems for the partisans. There was a small field hospital in their camp, with a few good Jewish doctors. But there was always a shortage of medicines and only primitive medical equipment. Forced to sleep in their clothes and boots, to be always ready for action, their bodies were rarely exposed to the air or washed, so they suffered from terrible skin conditions, rashes and boils.

As if this were not torment enough, the ever-present lice on their skin, in their hair and on their clothes caused endless suffering. Lice had an amazing ability to reproduce and outlive all attempts at eradication, and Leibke was forever scratching at the detested blood-sucking creatures. He learnt to tell the various types of lice apart either by their colour or the number of legs they had. He would not be rid of them until the end of the war.

For both the partisans and the families living in the forest, existence was extremely arduous. It was toughest on those aged under 15 or over 50, as they were less physically robust. Likewise, people from the cities, who had been used to greater home comforts, were less able than rural folk and villagers to handle the hardships and lack of amenities. For some, the primitive conditions and constant drain on their health proved too much and they succumbed. Even away from the murderous Nazis and their collaborators, life was precarious.

But despite these adversities, Leibke knew he had made the right choice in becoming a partisan. At last he felt fully and completely alive. He had an important purpose, fighting the enemy in ways which really counted. He was still afraid of being captured and tortured, but in common with his fellow fighters, he carried with him his own weapon of self-destruction: an anti-tank grenade. Each partisan was issued with one to use on himself in the event of capture, because a) captured partisans were not allowed an easy death, and b) under torture he might give away vital information. Leibke's grenade was fastened to his belt at all times and he found comfort in its presence as a last resort. (After his area was liberated in 1944 and he no longer needed the grenade, he decided to use it to catch fish. He pulled the pin and tossed it into a river but nothing happened. It turned out he had been carrying a dud grenade all along.)

As the war dragged on it took a tragic toll on Leibke's family. His brother Benjamin was killed in an ambush by Lithuanians, while on a mission to secure rifles for the defence of the small forest settlement to which he was moving with his sister Frieda and their father. They were inconsolable at his loss. Then, not long afterwards, Leibke heard the news he had been dreading for the past year: that his mother and grandmother had been deported from their ghetto to an extermination camp. He had dared to hope that somehow they would escape deportation, now he had to accept the reality that they were lost. His sadness was unbearable.

A few months later, in the autumn of 1943, Leibke's unit was moving through the area where his father and sister were living, so he decided to enter the forest and pay a visit to their family camp. They had a loving reunion and talked late into the night.

The next morning the camp's sentries brought in a local farmer they had caught lurking at the edge of the forest. He claimed he was only looking for a stray cow – which sounded reasonable enough – but something about him roused suspicion. Leibke's father was nervous but the others dismissed his fears and they let the farmer go.

It was a mistake. The man had betrayed them, no doubt for money or favours, and in the afternoon the camp was attacked by some 150 armed men. But they weren't Germans. From their uniforms and caps Leibke could tell they were Poles, members of the Home Army, a resistance group that was as anti-Semitic as it was anti-Nazi. Too lightly armed to fend them off, the Jews of the camp fled into the forest, pursued by their attackers.

Leibke's father was hit in the back with a dumdum bullet, which expands on impact in order to create a larger and more severe wound. Leibke held him up and helped him to a tree, then looked back and saw his sister running frantically towards them. She was being chased by three attackers. Leibke took aim and managed to shoot two of them, then his rifle jammed. 'Run Frieda, run!' he yelled. 'Faster!' But Frieda stumbled and fell, and he watched in horror as her pursuer caught up and ran her through, over and over, with his bayonet.

Leibke cried out in anguish as his sister's life was extinguished. But there was no time to stop. He and his father – his massive wound now haemorrhaging blood – had to get away before they too were killed.

They found brief sanctuary with a kindly farmer and Leibke settled his father in the barn. He did what he could to treat the wound and tried to keep up his father's will to live, but it was no use. Before he died he made Leibke promise never to forget who he was or where he came from and always to be proud of his Jewish heritage. 'I know you will survive, Leibke, and begin a new life when this is all over.

Tell your children and grandchildren about your family and what happened to us. And avenge us. Avenge your brother, your sister, your mother … and me. And all of our murdered people.'

When his life finally slipped away, Leibke cradled his father's thin body and wept. 'Papa don't leave me. What shall I do without you?' All of a sudden he felt utterly alone and forsaken. He was now the last remaining member of his family, a solitary link to what once was. His family's memories, its very soul, would reside solely with him.

As he buried his father in the forest, beside his brother Benjamin's grave, he knew that he was also burying the last piece of his childhood.

Leibke returned to his partisan brigade and continued to battle the Nazis and their collaborators in Lithuania, Poland and Belorussia, until the Russian army liberated those territories in June 1944. He was by then 19 years old and no longer the *patsan*, the little kid, but a seasoned partisan.

The time had come to fulfil his promise to his father. One night he paid a visit to the deceitful farmer who had betrayed the family camp to the Poles, causing the deaths of his father and sister. He smashed open the farmhouse door and confronted the terrified man. 'Say your prayers,' he ordered, ignoring the farmer's pleas for mercy. In a blind rage, reliving the terrible scene of his sister's death, Leibke stabbed him repeatedly with his bayonet.

He was sure he had killed the traitor but he learnt later that in fact the farmer had not died. Instead Leibke had inflicted a far worse punishment on him: he was so badly maimed that he lived the rest of his life unable to see, speak or function in any normal way.

Then Leibke returned to his home town of Eisiskes, where he hunted down many of the Lithuanians responsible for the murder of his relatives, friends and neighbours. Before long, they had all met their end in front of a firing squad.

At last the partisan's job was done. Leibke could put away his rifle, take off his bandolier and start to contemplate his future, the new post-war life his father had rightly predicted for him.

Chapter Three

Stephen Grady – The Boy who Messed with a Messerschmitt

Stephen Grady was well known as a mischief-maker in his small town of Nieppe in north-eastern France, on the Belgian border. He and his fellow scamps would deflate the tyres and loosen the saddles on the bicycles of grumpy old villagers, or else pelt their windows with mud balls. He also liked to knock on people's doors and run away.

One of his more daring escapades was the practical joke he played on the local brothel. He didn't really understand what went on inside but heard his father saying that the men who frequented it 'were only after one thing and needed to be taught a lesson'. So Stephen and his pal Roussel overturned the 50-gallon oil drum that served as the brothel's pissoir and flooded the place with urine. Then they fled laughing down the road, followed by screams and shouts and shaking fists.

Monsieur Ruckebusch, the strict headmaster at his Catholic school, despaired of him. On one occasion, after failing to own up to one of his misdemeanours, Stephen's entire class was made to write out 500 times: *I must not act without considering the consequences of my actions upon others*. Words which would later haunt him.

Stephen's father, Stephen Snr., was English. A British army corporal in the Great War, he had married a French woman and stayed on in France, working as a gardener for the Imperial War Graves Commission, tending the graves of fallen soldiers at Nieppe's military cemeteries. He missed his country profoundly, refused to learn French and tried to bring up his two boys and two girls – but especially his older son Stephen – to be English, like himself.

His small, frail mother had slowly been going blind, so in order to help run the household, her sister – Aunt Valentine – and mother moved into the cramped, rundown little house on the Rue du Sac, adjacent to the Pont d'Achelles war cemetery where his father spent most of his time toiling amongst the neat rows of uniform white headstones.

Every two years the Grady family would head for Calais and the ferry to Dover, and from there board a train to Ramsgate to spend a fortnight's holiday with Stephen's paternal grandmother. Stephen's dad would be in his element and the visits always made French-born, bilingual Stephen wish he were truly English. He loved the milkmen and the friendly bobbies, fish and chips, and crumpets, the magical shop called Woolworth's and Cadbury's chocolate bars in purple wrappers.

In the summer of 1937, shortly before their departure to England, 12-year-old Stephen was told he wouldn't be returning to France with his family after the holiday. He would instead be lodging with his gran at her bungalow in Pegwell Bay and attending St George's School in Ramsgate. Against his mother's wishes, his father insisted that he get away from little Nieppe and 'see the bigger picture'. Always up for an adventure, Stephen was only too willing.

Within a few weeks he began to feel at home in the strange new world of the English school system. He learnt to deal with pounds, shillings and pence, made local friends and laughed off their nickname for him of Froggy. Little by little, he learnt how to be English. So it came as a blow to him when the following year, at the end of his third term, a letter arrived from his parents summoning him home. In the end, apparently, his mother's will had prevailed.

Back in Nieppe, the family home now seemed even more overcrowded and uncomfortable. Stephen's mother had started using a white stick to help her get around and spent a lot of time praying with her rosary beads. His father spent his free hours glued to his primitive wireless set, straining to hear the (generally disquieting) news on the BBC Home Service. First there was Hitler's annexation of Austria, the Anschluss. Then came the annexation of the Sudetenland in Czechoslovakia, followed soon after by Kristallnacht, the Nazis' lethal pogrom against Germany's Jews. The Great War veteran wondered uneasily where it would all lead. Surely not another war?

But in the midst of all this anxiety and disappointment, there was a happy development in young Stephen's life. A new family, the Lombards, took over the farm down the road and their son Marcel was Stephen's age. They became best mates and before long were thick as thieves, tearing around the neighbourhood on their bicycles and getting up to various shenanigans. The Lombard farm became Stephen's second home and Monsieur Lombard was like a second father.

The two boys would spend hours sitting in the Lombards' hayloft, speculating on the future, the prospect of war and what exploits it might bring. Both planned military careers. Stephen was eager to join the British army and fire guns as his father did decades earlier. Marcel wanted to join the French air force and fly fighter planes.

On 1 September 1939 they heard an unfamiliar alarm sound in their village and saw Stephen's father cycling quickly in their direction. He screeched to a halt and yelled to his son to come home. When asked why, he explained the meaning of the 'tocsin alarm' the boys had heard: 'We must be at war with the Fritz, again.'

Stephen and Marcel looked at each other with wide-eyed excitement. *At last*! The potential for adventure now seemed boundless.

Less than a year later, in May 1940, Germany attacked France, quickly defeated the French army, chased the British Expeditionary Force off French soil via Dunkirk, and a sense of total catastrophe descended on the French population. The people of Nieppe panicked as the German army neared, and the town buzzed with rumours. In the surrounding area the sounds of exploding bombs and mortar filled the air. Then at the end of the month the first Wehrmacht troops appeared in the village. For a while a group of them were billeted at the Lombard farm.

Still up to their boyish pranks, Stephen and Marcel took to observing them secretly from behind a hedge. One day, armed with a brass fire extinguisher, they leapt up as a German soldier was passing by and blasted him at close range with a painful jet. The soldier cried out in alarm, shouted curses at them and tried to give chase but his way was blocked by the hedge. The teenaged pair dashed away gleefully through the fields.

But their greatest pleasure came from discovering abandoned weapons left behind by the hurriedly retreating French and British armies. Combing the woods, they found grenades, rifles, pistols and even light machine guns, along with the corresponding ammunition. They created a well-concealed hiding place for their arsenal, digging a pit beneath one of the two squat bastions flanking the Cross of Sacrifice in the Pont d'Achelles cemetery, reinforcing it with wooden planks and corrugated iron, and camouflaging the entrance.

A notice soon appeared outside the town hall declaring that anyone caught sabotaging German property or possessing arms of any kind faced the death penalty. Stephen's stomach churned as he read the notice and realised that he and Marcel could be shot for their buried cache of weapons. Their war games were growing very risky.

Shortly afterwards the kindly mayor of Nieppe, Monsieur Houcke, turned up at the Gradys' door with a stark warning: the Germans were asking whether there were any British living in the town, because as enemies of the Reich they were due for imprisonment and deportation. As the only family member not to have French papers, Stephen's father would have to go into hiding. This meant he would be unable to work and the family would be left without an income. But the mayor had a solution. Stephen could take over his father's gardening work in the cemeteries, for which the town council would pay him a modest salary. And so, aged 15, he became the family breadwinner. Meanwhile the embittered head of the household sought refuge with friends in a nearby town … when he wasn't 'in hiding' in the attic of his own house.

As the months passed, food and other daily necessities became scarce and real hardships began. The Germans were requisitioning the produce of local farmers, as well as all kinds of other essential goods, shipping them by the trainload to the Reich for the benefit of their own people.

On a sunny afternoon in June 1941 Stephen and Marcel were relaxing on the grass at the Lombard farm, musing on which of their favourite foods (all now unavailable) they would most like to eat, when their attention was suddenly diverted to the sky over their heads and they immediately lost interest in food. Two fighter planes roared into view – a Hurricane and a Messerschmitt – and a dogfight commenced. Climbing and diving, spiralling around each other with machine guns clattering, they battled it out until eventually one of them spluttered and came down with a trail of black smoke. It was the Messerschmitt. And in the distance the boys spotted a parachute opening and billowing down to earth.

Wasting no time, they hopped onto their bicycles and sped off in the direction of the downed plane. The chance to get a close look at this hated instrument of the Luftwaffe, broken and defeated, was irresistible.

They tracked it down to a potato field where it lay, ignominiously riddled with bullet holes, its propeller blades bent out of shape. Surrounding it was a small gathering of onlookers, plus a pair of German soldiers clutching machine guns.

Stephen and Marcel, partners in crime, grinned at each other as they casually strolled away. Their plan was to return with some tools at first light the following morning, when there would be no one around. The Messerschmitt offered rich pickings for the souvenir hunter.

At dawn they crept back to the plane. Prising open the cockpit canopy, they took turns sitting inside, playing with the control column and the instrument panel with its magnificent array of dials and switches, knobs and gauges. Then with pliers and screwdrivers Stephen set about removing a few instruments to take home as trophies. Once finished with that, he began to smash up the rest of the instrument panel.

But Marcel was growing edgy. He kept looking towards the nearby road and listening for the sound of approaching vehicles. Any moment now the Bosch might be coming back to retrieve their plane. 'Hurry up,' he urged his friend. 'We have to leave.'

Climbing out of the cockpit on to the wing, the patriotic Stephen had another brainwave. With his screwdriver he etched a message in large letters along the length of the fuselage: *vivent les aviateurs anglais qui ont abattu ce sale boche.* Translation: 'long live the English airmen who shot down this filthy Kraut'.

'You sure that's a good idea?' asked Marcel.

'Of course.'

'Please, Stéphane, let's go. We've done enough.'

But Stephen set himself one final task: to dislodge the big black cross on one of the plane's wings. What a prize! However, it was taking longer than he thought. There were so many rivets...

'*Merde*,' whispered a terrified Marcel. Stephen glanced up.

A black military staff car had appeared and was slowly bumping its way along the dirt track towards them. Behind it rumbled a big grey recovery lorry. The Nazis had arrived.

Two days of being locked in a filthy cell without food and water but with occasional beatings, followed by signed confessions, resulted in a harsh sentence for their act of sabotage against Reich property: incarceration 'for an indefinite period' at Loos Prison. Stephen had heard about that dilapidated, disease-ridden hellhole near Lille – it was where they banged up murderers and other hardened criminals. And yet the boys were lucky. Their youth saved them from an even worse fate: deportation to a German concentration camp, or a firing squad. As they sat hunched in the back of a police van, Stephen recalled that his headmaster Monsieur Ruckebusch had warned him, more than once, that his silly pranks would end in tears. And it was his fault that his best friend was in this terrible plight with him. He murmured an apology to Marcel.

'You never listen to me,' came the muted response.

Stephen was also anxious about his family. If as a result of his arrest the police searched his house and found his father hiding in the attic, that would be bad enough. But if they were to snoop around and discover the big cache of weapons buried in the war cemetery, surely that would mean a death sentence for them all. He ached with remorse. *I must not act without considering the consequences of my actions upon others ... .*

The boys were put into the German-run part of Loos Prison, reserved for political detainees: enemies of the Reich. Here conditions were even worse than Stephen had anticipated. Mouldy and rat-infested, reeking of human waste and unwashed bodies, he was separated from Marcel and shoved into a small cell with three emaciated prisoners and only one bed between the four of them. He sank down miserably in a corner beside the revolting toilet.

Meals were comprised of the 'soup' sploshed into each man's mess tin – a foul-smelling liquid with a few measly haricot beans floating on top – and a lump of black bread so rock hard it was almost impossible to chew. For sleeping, there were straw mattresses infested with fleas.

In the gloom of this fetid cell Stephen contemplated his uncertain future. How worried his parents must be about him; did they even know where he was? His wraith-like cellmates informed him about the death row cells on the floor below. From there, condemned prisoners were ultimately dragged away to be shot or deported. The fortunate ones were sentenced to five years' slave labour in Germany.

As the weeks passed he grew thinner and weaker; he felt he must be starting to resemble the other wretches in his cell. But on some days they could hear the unmistakable drone of Allied bombers overhead and that encouraging sound – a confirmation that the fight against the Nazis continued – was what gave them all hope.

Three months after his arrest, the cell door opened and a guard called his name. He was led into a prison office where he found Marcel, looking shockingly thin and pale. They were made to sign release papers, warned never to cause trouble again and told they were free to go. Amazingly, they were then handed back their bicycles. The big prison gates swung open and the two boys cycled away towards home in the warm sunshine, through the clean country air. How beautiful the world looked. The wind in their faces, they tossed their heads back and laughed.

Stephen arrived home in the Rue du Sac to find, to his great relief, that the family was well. His father was safe and the weapons stash remained undisturbed. All the women of the household – his mother, aunt, grandmother and two sisters – wept with happiness when he appeared on the doorstep, albeit shocked by his shrunken appearance.

They treated the famished boy to an array of precious foods they had been saving for a special occasion – a tin of baked beans, a hunk of cheese, some baked ham, bread with strawberry jam – all of which he devoured until he felt sick and had to hurry outside, where he vomited it all up.

Later, as he fell into bed for a very long sleep, he told himself he would never again endanger the lives of his loved ones. He would go back to his work in the cemeteries and stay out of trouble, thankful simply to be alive and free.

He soon learned how his release from Loos Prison had come about. Apparently Monsieur Faure, a crotchety old codger whose windows Stephen used to pelt with mud balls, had spotted the boys sitting in the Germans' lorry right after their arrest and alerted the mayor, Monsieur Jules Houcke, who in turn informed the Gradys. This gave his father a chance to leave home quickly and hide elsewhere. The mayor then began a lengthy process of pulling strings and vouching for the good character of the boys and their families. The determined intervention by the mayor of Nieppe, a respected local dignitary whose cooperation the German authorities wished to retain, eventually bore fruit.

What the Germans didn't realise was that Mayor Houcke (along with his brother Marcel) was a leading figure in the local resistance organisation, the *Voix du Nord,* Voice of the North. And in due course he came knocking at the Gradys' door in order to speak to Stephen. He pulled the boy aside and asked him whether he would like to 'make a contribution' to the war effort.

'I certainly would.'

'Good. Because there's something I'd like you to do.'

Stephen felt a ripple of excitement. He had been utterly deflated since his incarceration, feeling that he was merely marking time whilst the war was going on around him. Maybe now he could get actively involved.

Houcke explained that his organisation ran an escape route for Allied airmen being shot down in the area. They helped the airmen avoid capture by hiding them in the homes of trusted sympathisers and arranging their hazardous onward journey across France, into neutral Switzerland or Spain, and so back to England. But their task had recently got much harder. Aware of the escape line's existence, the Germans were trying to infiltrate it, find out how it worked and who was involved, in order to destroy it. To this end they had started parachute-dropping their own agents posing as downed Allied air crew, so that they would be taken into the care of the *Voix du Nord*.

These German agents spoke excellent English and were very clever. They had learnt the manners and argot of Allied airmen and acquired the necessary background knowledge needed to dupe members of the French Resistance. But they would find it harder to fool a native English-speaker, someone like Stephen who was half-English and had even attended school in England. He could quiz any airmen claiming to have bailed out in their vicinity and distinguish between the genuine and the fake. Of course, if he got it wrong – if a single German agent succeeded in infiltrating the escape chain – the consequences for them all would be dire. It was a huge responsibility. And he was still only 17.

He agreed at once.

Houcke told him he must prepare three separate lists of test questions: one for British air crew, one for Americans and one for Canadians. He would have to do research and devise probing questions of the kind that only a true native of that country would be able to answer. And if he decided someone was an imposter, that person would be 'dealt with'.

Eager though he was to start unmasking German spies, it was an altogether different role which fell upon him first. Houcke summoned him to a secret meeting of his resistance cell: a handful of middle-aged men who had served in the Great War and, too old to fight now, were itching to get back at the Bosch in other ways. Stephen could tell they were not much pleased to find a raw youth in their midst, especially one with a reputation for mischief-making. Could he be trusted or would the known prankster get them all killed?

Houcke assigned everyone a code name; Stephen's was Iroquois. And he outlined their tasks: besides assisting Allied airmen, they would distribute a clandestine anti-Nazi newspaper, also named *La Voix du Nord*, and undertake occasional acts of sabotage.

'We must have weapons,' announced one of the others, a headmaster called Monsieur Cornette. 'With this dangerous work we need guns to protect ourselves.'

Houcke explained that there were no weapons to be had in Nieppe, as the Germans had confiscated them all.

'Without guns we're a laughing stock,' said Cornette.

The men brooded over their dilemma.

Then Stephen piped up. 'Excuse me, but I have weapons.'

'Really?' sneered Cornette. 'Do you mean the peashooter you use on the congregation in church?'

'I have guns,' insisted Stephen.

Now Mayor Houcke spoke. 'Please tell us about your guns, Stéphane.'

The teenager proceeded to itemise the weapons in the hoard he had amassed, still safely buried in the Pont d'Achelles cemetery: Fusils Lebel and Fusils Gras rifles, Mousquetons and Modèles 36 rifles, a Browning pistol and brand new light machine gun with tripod, plus ammunition, grenades, flares.

Which is how Stephen became the cell's arms supplier.

A delighted Houcke gave him permission to recruit his own small sub-group within the resistance organisation – but only those individuals he would trust with his life. Naturally his first recruit was his best mate, Marcel Lombard. Then he picked two others. Francis André, an engineering student who had worked in his father's bicycle repair shop in Nieppe, was a good friend and had a reputation for fearlessness. And Maurice Leblon, a young factory worker and Anglophile, whose family had already risked all by sheltering an English soldier earlier in the war. They dubbed themselves the Four Musketeers.

The *Voix* instructed Stephen to make his way to an address in a nearby village. When he arrived, he found an imposing villa and was met by its suave owner, a man in his thirties called Jean Sonneville. His luxurious home was adorned with antiques, beautiful paintings and tapestries.

Stephen gazed around in awe; he had never been anywhere like it. But why was he there?

As he was to find out, Sonneville had been a successful smuggler before the war. Now he was part of a resistance organisation called the War Office, or WO, headed by a young British army officer whom everyone referred to simply as Capitaine Michel. The Capitaine had been parachuted into France by the SOE in order to build a resistance network in the Lille area and coordinate sabotage activities.

Sonneville told Stephen that the WO was now working together with the *Voix du Nord*. Then he led Stephen out to a large garden behind his house and through the field beyond to a shed. Inside were two Canadian airmen who claimed their bomber had been shot down by German flak. So this was to be his debut life-or-death mission to unmask potential imposters – .only he didn't have his Canadian test questions with him.

They were the first Allied airmen he had ever met – a squadron leader and his navigator – and the three of them began an informal conversation, a little stilted at first. The Canadians were amused to find themselves being appraised by such a young interrogator. Mostly interested in discussing French women, they feigned amazement to discover that the teenaged Stephen had had little personal experience of them.

They chatted for a while. With no questionnaire to go by, Stephen relied on instinct. He made up his mind quickly.

'I'm pretty sure they're genuine,' he told Sonneville.

'Good. I agree.'

His next mission was less straightforward. A farmer had been sheltering a British airman called Malcolm Whiting, whom he had discovered tangled in a tree. Whiting said he was the navigator of a Halifax bomber shot down during a night raid. When Stephen arrived at the isolated farmhouse he found a tall moustachioed young man in a tattered uniform.

He seemed almost *too* English, a bit of a caricature with his 'old chap' and 'oh cripes'. A nervous Stephen launched into his list of simple questions on everyday matters any reasonably savvy Englishmen should be able to answer.

Whiting knew that the statue of Eros was in Piccadilly Circus. He could quote the advertising slogan 'Guinness is good for you'. And in answer to 'Whose works are performed by the D'Oyly Carte Opera Company?' he replied correctly: 'Gilbert and Sullivan'. And so they carried on, with questions about cricket terminology, the FA Cup and English railway journeys. Whiting gave a smooth performance. But behind the airman's steady gaze, Stephen sensed something else going on. What was the man thinking? He knew he had to get this right. So many lives were at stake.

After 'Iroquois' had run through his questionnaire, Whiting mentioned that he'd been lucky to bail out successfully from his flaming aircraft and survive; the rest of his crew were all dead.

'Well,' observed Stephen, 'you seem quite cheerful, considering.'

For a moment Whiting looked at him in silence. Then, in a more sombre tone he told Stephen not to confuse his light-hearted manner with cheerfulness. It was simply that having been through a terrifying experience in which he lost his six closest chums and nearly died himself, it was only a determined lightness which kept him from caving in. 'I don't suppose you can understand, because you are too young and you're insulated from the war.'

Insulated? If only Whiting knew of his harrowing three months in Loos Prison. And the chronic food and fuel shortage, his dangerous missions and his constant fear.

He had seen and heard enough to know that Whiting was the real McCoy. But the interview was only the first part of his undertaking. Now he had to lead the airman to the next safehouse in the escape chain. They had many kilometres to cover by bicycle before the curfew and there might be German roadblocks on the way.

'I've brought you some farmer's overalls to wear over your uniform,' he told the airman. 'Stay a couple of hundred metres behind me at all times. If I see a roadblock ahead I'll signal you by taking a white handkerchief out of my pocket and dropping it. Then you try hard to disappear.'

If the worst happened and they were captured, Whiting would be sent to a PoW camp in Germany to sit out the rest of the war. Stephen would be shot for trying to help him escape.

Over the following weeks he interviewed a number of American airmen and grew familiar with the Yanks' swagger and gum-chewing insouciance, their instant friendliness, gargantuan appetites and lack of sophistication. But even so, John McGuire stood out.

'I'll be glad to see him go,' said the gruff farmer in whose hayloft McGuire had been hiding. 'He won't stop eating. He's practically finished our food supplies!'

Stephen climbed the ladder to the hayloft and met the towering, tough-looking airman. 'Hello, I am Iroquois. How are you?'

'Hungry as hell,' replied McGuire. 'These Frenchies have been starving me ever since I got here.'

After explaining that like most locals, the farmer and his family had barely enough for themselves, Stephen launched into his carefully compiled questions.

'Who gave America the Statue of Liberty?'

McGuire narrowed his eyes. 'Search me.'

'Who wrote *Rhapsody in Blue*?'

'No idea.'

'How many states are there in the USA?'

'I know that one – forty-eight!' And after a pause: 'How did I do? Am I top of the class?' He was treating the whole thing as a joke. But Stephen reckoned no German could play a Yank quite as well as McGuire played himself, so he handed him a pair overalls and told him about their long cycle ride back to Nieppe.

'What? I haven't ridden a bike since I was a kid.'

'You're going to have to ride one now because it's your only chance of avoiding a German prison camp.'

A few minutes later the airman was gamely wobbling down the road behind Stephen. 'I think I got it!' he yelled. 'As long as there ain't any sharp corners!'

Stephen groaned. He prayed the Yank wouldn't get them both arrested.

After several uneventful kilometres they were approaching a small town. As Stephen rounded a corner he was confronted by a large column of German soldiers marching down the road. With no time to drop the handkerchief, he frantically wondered what to do. But there was really no choice; he just had to keep on going and hope for the best.

A minute later he had passed the column, and a little further on he glanced discreetly over his shoulder. To his great relief he saw McGuire still riding behind him. The American waved and smiled, having blithely cycled past the first Wehrmacht soldiers he had ever clapped eyes on and looking for all the world like a rustic Frenchman out on his daily errands.

A week later he got a message from the *Voix du Nord* telling him that a Canadian pilot had bailed out in the area and was holed up in a village nearby. He was told that no wreckage had been found and the poor traumatised airman couldn't remember where he had hidden his parachute.

The good-natured farmer who had been harbouring him led Stephen to an outbuilding. Inside in semi-darkness was a man who introduced himself as Lieutenant Eastwood of the Royal Canadian Air Force. He wanted to know who 'Iroquois' worked for.

'I work for myself.'

'So, it is kind of you to come.'

A polite fellow, thought Stephen.

They sat down opposite each other and Stephen read out the first question on his Canadian questionnaire. 'What is the motto of the Royal Canadian Air Force?'

'It is *per ardua ad astra*, same as the RAF's.'

'What year did your air force become royal?'

'In 1924.'

'And who is its Inspector General?'

'Air Vice Marshal Croil.'

'Correct.' Stephen began to trust Eastwood. But then through the gloomy light he noticed that one of the airman's knees was trembling and he was clasping his thighs tightly. He decided to carry on a bit longer.

'Just another couple of questions, then. Let's see … what's the difference between a Yale and a Harvard?'

'Ha! That is a trick question, is it not?' Eastwood's laughter sounded forced. 'Everybody knows they are universities of America.'

Stephen smiled back at him. The first two Canadian airmen he had questioned, in Sonneville's shed, had told him that every RCAF pilot would know the names of their two training aircraft and the differences between them. Eastwood couldn't have forgotten this, even with the stress of being shot down.

'Next question. What's a yellow doughnut?' A genuine RCAF pilot would tell him it was slang for an airman's dinghy.

By now both both of Eastman's legs were trembling and his face looked sweaty. 'I cannot be sure … I think it is a lemon cake.' Another hollow laugh.

'One final question. How does an airman become a member of the Caterpillar Club?' (Answer: by bailing out of a plane.)

Eastwood's nerves were now impossible to disguise and he held his head in his hands. 'I am sure I know that.' He pulled at his hair. 'Is it a club for people who are still learners to fly, who have not yet got their wings?'

'Yes, quite right, Lieutenant Eastwood,' said Stephen briskly. 'Thank you.' He stood up. 'Don't worry, we'll soon have you on your way back to your squadron. I'll arrange for our transport. Please wait here until I come back for you.'

'Good, good.' Eastwood nodded, uneasily.

Hurrying back to the farmhouse, Stephen told the farmer that the man he was hiding was a German agent. 'But you must continue to look after him as if you didn't know. Bring him his meals, be pleasant. If he thinks you suspect him, he'll kill you. I will inform our organisation and they will quickly take care of it.' With that he cycled away.

Back in Nieppe, Stephen reported his verdict to Mayor Houcke.

'You're quite sure, Stéphane?'

'As sure as I can be.'

'Very well. You have done your job, now we will do ours.'

Later that day, as he was carrying out his duties in the war cemetery, Stephen reflected on the enemy spy called 'Eastwood'. Perhaps he was already dead. In any case there would be no dignified resting place for him, no headstone with his name on it, which his family could visit with flowers. The would-be infiltrator would simply be 'disappeared'.

Shortly after his unmasking of the bogus pilot, Sonneville invited Stephen to join him on a hush-hush mission, and he took Maurice along, one of the Four Musketeers. The three of them set off one morning in an old lorry powered by a smoky gazogène – a primitive charcoal-burning stove – to a mysterious destination. But first they they stopped off at a turnip field, where they loaded turnips into the back of the lorry, and then at a farm to collect bales of straw. After this they met up with the Houcke brothers, who were driving another gazogène lorry, and Sonneville explained that they would be travelling in convoy to the village of Ransart, south of Arras. Ever more intriguing.

When the antiquated lorries finally pulled up sluggishly in the village square in Ransart, Stephen and Maurice watched in dread as a man wearing the uniform of the notoriously pro-Nazi Vichy Security Police approached the Houckes' lorry and got in. They then drove off, with Sonneville's lorry following. Stephen and Maurice exchanged stunned glances. What on earth was going on?

The two vehicles drove down a deserted country track and into a field, where they juddered to a halt and everybody got out. The Vichy policeman, armed and looking purposeful, strode towards the two apprehensive boys. But he merely greeted Stephen in a perfect English accent and shook his hand. 'Hello, Iroquois. People call me Capitaine Michel.'

For a moment Stephen was too shocked to speak. He had long hoped to meet this legendary SOE operative. Now he didn't know what to say.

'It's an honour,' he murmured. 'God save the King.'

'Yes. And *vive la France libre!*'

And so to the mission at hand. They set about recovering a wealth of weaponry airdropped by the RAF. Hidden in a silo were three large capsules, each containing several aluminium drums. The Capitaine opened one up, took out a Sten gun and showed the others how to use it. They were each allotted one for the return journey.

The heavy drums were loaded on to the lorries and covered with turnips and straw. Then the gazogènes were fired up once more and they headed back towards Nieppe, with Stephen and Maurice valiantly 'riding shotgun' atop their turnips, their Stens tucked away in the straw by their side.

Stephen had been growing apart from his family, in whom he knew he could not confide, both for their safety and that of others. His parents suspected he was involved in dangerous activities and feared for him; they were too afraid, in fact, to want to know the details. And the more distance Stephen felt from the members of his own household, the closer he grew to that other family, his comrades in the Resistance. And especially to Sonneville, whose house became another home to him. They would sit for hours in the warmth of his kitchen, discussing the war, eating and drinking and smoking cigarettes. The ex-smuggler always had plenty of everything.

And from Sonneville he learned more about Capitaine Michel. That he was born in Brighton to an Irish mother and French father, was partly schooled in France and spoke the language like a native. (Hence his successful disguise as a Vichy policeman.) That he had been wounded at Dunkirk and the following year was recruited into the SOE and parachuted into France, but was captured along with other operatives and imprisoned in a Vichy concentration camp in the Dordogne. Undaunted, he organised a mass escape of British officers, leading them across the Pyrenees to Spain and from there back to England. But in due course he returned to France to set up and run the new SOE network based in Lille, and had been carrying out sabotage missions of breathtaking audacity. He had blown up trains and factories, naval depots and wharves and – his *pièce de résistance*, in a particularly apt use of the phrase – the locomotive works at Fives, one of the most important in France, putting them out of action for two months. An action hero straight out of *Boys' Own*. The furious Germans were now looking for him everywhere.

Stephen met the intrepid Capitaine Michel again a few days later at the barn where the drums from the Ransart drop were being stored. The arms were to be divided up between their two resistance groups; as well as the Sten guns there were pistols, bombs and grenades.

Stephen sat next to the Capitaine as he unwrapped and examined some explosives. 'Have you ever shot anyone?' he asked the teenager.

'No.'

He handed Stephen a Luger pistol. 'Then here's what you need to know: only two shots, one to the stomach and one to the heart. And don't look at his face.'

Stephen gave a tentative nod.

'If we're captured they'll torture us and in the end we might talk. Then they'll kill us anyway. Better to die first. So make sure you always have one last bullet for yourself in case you need it.'

'I hope that time never comes,' said Stephen, studying the Luger.

'Me too. But let's continue to be brave, so that we inspire bravery in others.'

Reaching into another of the drums, filled with NAAFI goods, the Capitaine pulled out packs of cigarettes, bars of chocolate and a box of tea. He handed them to Stephen and said they were for his parents, because he had no idea what torment they went through every time he left his house.

Stephen never saw the heroic SOE agent again. In November 1943 a member of his resistance group was captured and under torture gave away the address of Capitaine Michel's safehouse in Lille. Early the next morning the house was surrounded by a large raiding party of soldiers led by an inspector of the German field police, who banged loudly on the door. Firing through the door the Capitaine shot and killed the police inspector and wounded one of the soldiers, before trying to escape from the rear exit. He died in a burst of gunfire. He was 29 years old. And his real name was Michael Trotobas.

But the war, and Stephen's part in it, went on. His next assignment was to escort five American airmen – crew members of a Flying Fortress – from a village on the Belgian border to La Bassée, 30 kilometres away along a road well known for being used by German soldiers. Monsieur Bouchery, a well-liked local dignitary and *Voix du Nord* operative in La Bassée, had agreed to harbour the Americans until they could be moved further along the escape route. Stephen was to guide one airman there per day until all five were safely delivered.

On the third day he arrived at Bouchery's house and saw, to his horror, the two previously escorted Americans relaxing outside in broad daylight as though on holiday. He quickly ushered them indoors. Didn't they realise that a German patrol might pass by at any moment? And that equally dangerous French collaborators could be anywhere? The Yanks were contrite, like chastised schoolboys. But even worse, Stephen learned that the previous evening the bored airmen had persuaded Bouchery to let them go out for a few drinks at a local café. Unbelievably reckless.

So it was with immense relief that Stephen completed his mission. Luckily they had not been stopped at a roadblock; all five airmen were now in place and ready to be moved along the chain by another resistance cell.

But a couple of days later Stephen was shocked to learn from Marcel Houcke that the Gestapo had arrested the five airmen at Lille railway station. 'An informer must have observed them at the café that night and reported them to the police.'

'And Bouchery?'

'His house was raided and they took him away, along with his family.' Houcke gazed sadly at his young ally. 'You used only your code name?'

'Yes.'

'And no one followed you back to Nieppe?'

Stephen shook his head.

'Then you are safe. They are probably torturing Bouchery for names right now.'

There were further bold feats in store for Stephen, now a young man of 18. Besides vetting and escorting more Allied airmen there were acts of railway sabotage inspired by Sonneville, using explosives from the Ransart drop. He also helped to spring Mayor Houcke from prison, following his arrest by the Vichy police for issuing false identity cards enabling young Frenchmen to evade forced labour in Germany. (The police were unaware of his far more serious Resistance activities.)

It was perhaps inevitable that the time would come for him to be required to kill someone. He was chosen by Sonneville to assassinate a German officer called Hans, who had been conducting an affair with the daughter of a café owner in a neighbouring village. Hans worked for the Todt Organisation at one of its military engineering projects on the northern coast of France, but at weekends took the train down to visit his girlfriend. He had been overheard making drunken boasts about knowing the identities of local Resistance members and was threatening to expose them. Clearly this could not be allowed to happen.

At first Stephen balked at carrying out the assassination. He wouldn't mind gunning down German soldiers in battle. But shooting one in cold blood? A year or two earlier it would have been utterly impossible. But a lot had happened to him since then. Reluctantly he accepted the mission. If the lives of brave Resistance members were at stake, Hans would have to be eliminated.

On the allotted day, Stephen received confirmation that the German soldier was at the café. He left his bicycle in a neighbouring alley and released the safety catch on the Luger hidden in his coat pocket. Then he walked over to the café and went inside. It was empty. But a moment later the owner, a plump older woman, emerged through a door at the back and asked Stephen what he wanted.

He ordered a beer and sat down at a table. When it was brought to him he calmly took a couple of sips before asking the *patronne* nonchalantly: 'Is the German officer here?'

She was standing behind the bar, from where she had been eyeing him warily.

'What do you want with him?'

'I'm looking for work. I thought he might know of something on the coast.'

After a moment she called out: 'Hans, there's a young man here who wants to ask you about work.' A tall blond man in his thirties appeared from the back room. He didn't much resemble a dangerous Nazi officer, in his off-duty shirtsleeves and corduroy trousers. Hans perched on a barstool, folded his arms and looked at Stephen genially. 'What is it you're after?'

For an instant Stephen was tempted to hurry away and forget his mission. Then he reminded himself that Hans was in fact a deadly enemy. He stood up and pulled out the Luger. Remembering the Capitaine's words, he fired once at the stomach and once at the heart; the gunshots were unexpectedly loud. And although he didn't mean to, he couldn't stop himself from looking at Hans's face as he cried out; it was distorted with shock and rage. Then he crumpled.

A moment later Stephen was back on his bicycle, speeding away into the night as the *patronne's* horrified shrieking faded in the distance behind him. Back at Sonneville's house he didn't feel gratified or elated, only empty and numb.

When the long-awaited D-Day landings took place in June 1944, the people of Nieppe could at last believe their salvation was at hand. During the course of the summer the Wehrmacht gradually retreated from the area. The last remaining soldiers, weary and dejected, were only too willing to surrender to the Resistance. Even teenaged Stephen, rifle over his shoulder, marched a column of them down the road to captivity.

But the SS, fanatical to end, would not give up. In early September they arrived to blow up the bridge over the River Lys at Pont de Nieppe, which an army of Resistance fighters was trying to protect so that the Allies could use the crucial crossing point. The SS slaughtered most of the defenders and destroyed the bridge.

Many of Stephen's friends were killed that day, including his childhood pal Roussel, with whom – in another lifetime, it seemed – he had flooded the town brothel with an overturned pissoir. Marcel

Houcke, shot in the foot, survived by submerging himself in the river and breathing through a reed. Stephen only just escaped the carnage, sprinting down streets and clambering over rooftops, chased by machine-gun fire.

For two days he hid in a dank and dirty car repair shop, listening to the distant sounds of shooting and explosions. But on the third morning all was quiet. The Germans had gone. And a day later the first British soldiers arrived. He was free.

Chapter Four

Truus and Freddie Oversteegen – Sisters in Arms

Truus and Freddie were Dutch sisters growing up in the 1930s in Haarlem. Sandwiched between the capital Amsterdam and the long stretch of sand dunes along the country's north-western coastline, the medieval city had been famous since the seventeenth century as the centre of the country's tulip-growing industry. Dazzling multicoloured tulip fields lay to the north and south of them.

But they were a poor family, scraping along on meagre state handouts. The girls' parents had divorced when they were small – unusual for those days – and they lived with their single mother, a strong-willed woman with communist affiliations who instilled a fervent socialism in her daughters. It was a passion born of the great Depression, a time of mass unemployment and poverty, long dole queues, protests and demonstrations.

With the rise of Hitler in 1933, the family was confronted with a new enemy and by the following year they were sharing their humble home with refugees smuggled out of Nazi Germany: Jews, communists and other political dissidents. It had to be done surreptitiously because the Dutch government prohibited such private actions; if discovered, these illegal 'lodgers' were deported back to Germany, where a prison sentence or the new concentration camp at Dachau awaited them. Truus and Freddie learned at an early age to keep quiet about what was going on in their private lives, because talking could be dangerous.

In 1938, when Truus was 14 years old, she left school and started working long hours as a live-in domestic servant. Her modest earnings were desperately needed for the family: her mother, 12-year-old sister Freddie and their much younger half-brother Robbie. But for a teenager with forthright socialist inclinations, skivvying in the homes of wealthy capitalists was a particularly bad fit. Her jobs tended not to last very long.

And then came the war, Holland's hopeless attempt at staying neutral, and invasion by the Wehrmacht during the blitzkrieg of spring 1940. The 'terror bombing' of Rotterdam on 14 May was so devastating – 1,000 killed, 85,000 made homeless and the levelling of the city centre – that the country was compelled to surrender the following day and fall under German occupation.

Truus, 16, and 14-year-old Freddie became active in distributing Holland's key underground anti-Nazi publications: *De Vonk* (The Spark), founded by the resistance member and pioneering gay rights campaigner Nico Engelschman; *De Waarheid* (The Truth), the paper of the Communist Party of the Netherlands, and a youth magazine called *De Koevoet* (The Crowbar), founded by the anti-fascist youth movement leader Kees Boekman. Through the latter they began to take part in some more lively, hands-on activities. For their mother, it was only to be expected that her teenage daughters, as true 'comrades', would take part in the struggle against the occupation despite the obvious risks involved.

One evening at a group meeting at Kees Boekman's home, after his wife Bep had put their two small children to bed, Kees announced that they would be having some fun the following night. Anton Mussert, leader of the pro-Nazi Dutch National Socialist Movement, the NSB, and as such the country's most prominent fascist, would be holding a public rally in Haarlem. 'Boys and girls,' said Kees, 'let's spoil his big meeting. We'll get some cutters and cut the wires of his microphone.' He urged Truus, Freddie and the others to encourage high school pupils to attend the meeting *en masse* and make their anti-Mussert feelings known.

The following night a gratifyingly large crowd of boys and girls arrived at the rally, on their bicycles as requested. Mussert approached the podium to speak and at a given signal the youngsters all started sounding their bicycle bells. Then two members of Kees's group ran up to the stage and cut the microphone wires. As the diminutive

Dutch *führer* carried on speaking without sound, everyone roared with laughter. And the bells kept on ringing cheerfully. But now the NSB's paramilitary wing, the *Weerbaarheidsafdeling* (known as the WA) – who had been standing guard on the periphery – sprang into action, beating up youngsters in the crowd and smashing their bikes. There was a scramble to escape the violence and the rally came to an early end. Mussert had been unable to disseminate his hateful ideology.

'Ha! Now he can go hide behind his auntie's arse!' shouted one of the teenage protesters.

Everyone knew Anton Mussert was married to his maternal aunt, the much older Maria.

Late one night there was a knock on the Oversteegens' door. Everyone froze. Any unexpected visit could end in disaster. It was a Friday and the small group of Jews currently hiding in their home were in the room above, celebrating Sabbath. Truus and Freddie sat and waited anxiously as their mother answered the door.

She led two men into the living room. To the family's relief, they were clearly not policemen. One worked for the Resistance and he explained that the frightened-looking man with him, whose name was Arie, was being sought by the authorities and needed a hiding place. Could they help? There was a long discussion and it was finally agreed that Truus would accompany Arie to an address in central Haarlem, the home of sympathisers. They should walk arm in arm, like close relatives, so as to avoid suspicion. It was vital that they were not followed.

Truus put her clothes on and they headed off into the night. She found walking in an intimate manner with this older stranger awkward and embarrassing. But tense and sweating, she guided him along the route as her mission demanded … until she glanced backwards and saw a man walking close behind them. 'Run!' she urged the panic-stricken Arie. They tore down the street, ducked through a small gate between two houses, ran hand-in-hand through an alley, then through another gate and down another alley, on and on, until out of breath and lungs bursting they sank to the ground beside a wall to rest. They waited.

The man was gone. Silently, Arie took Truus's hand and kissed it. More embarrassment. She quickly pulled her hand away and got up. 'Come on, let's go.'

They arrived at the safehouse and as instructed gave the two long and one short rings on the doorbell. Inside was a kindly married couple, shopkeepers who lived above their small radio repair shop. They agreed to take the fugitive in until further arrangements could be made for him.

'Goodbye Arie,' said Truus, 'and good luck.'

Leaving the house, she was relieved to find the street empty, and cautiously made her way back home, telling her mother that all had gone 'very well'.

Some time later they heard that everyone at the safehouse had been arrested. The shopkeeper couple were never seen again. As for Arie, he was said to have jumped from the train on which he was being deported but he couldn't outrun the Holocaust. When Truus heard of his death she recalled with a stab of remorse his grateful kiss on her hand. If only she had been kinder.

It wasn't long before the Oversteegen sisters came to the attention of Frans van der Wiel, commander of the Haarlem Council of Resistance. One evening in the summer of 1941, the tall, debonair Dutchman, wearing a neat grey suit, turned up at their home and asked to speak to the girls alone. He had a proposition for them.

The three seated themselves in the living room. 'We've heard a lot about you and know that you are not cowards,' Frans began. 'So would you like to join our secret army? We have weapons with which to fight the Germans. But if you join us, you must promise not to talk about this with anyone, not even your mother. Can you promise that?'

They nodded. It all sounded irresistibly exciting.

'We'll be carrying out sabotage – blowing up bridges and railways – and we'll need to steal weapons from the Germans. On occasion we'll be forced to shoot. You'll have to learn how to fire a gun, plant a bomb and throw a hand grenade.' He paused as he lit a cigarette and looked at each of them in turn. 'Could you shoot and kill someone?'

Freddie was taken was aback and hesitated. 'I've never done that before,' she admitted somewhat superfluously, staring at her small childlike hands.

Truus was more self-assured. 'Yes, if I really have to,' she declared. 'If he was a fascist swine who drags people from their homes and has them executed.' Then a moment later: 'But how can you tell if he's one of the evil ones? Not all German soldiers are committed Nazis, after all.'

'Don't worry about that. When we shoot to kill it will be someone from the Gestapo, or else a Dutch traitor who betrays his own countrymen to the enemy. Those are the bastards we're after.'

Freddie turned to her sister with mounting enthusiasm: 'Are we going to do it?'

Truus deliberated for a moment before nodding. 'Okay we will join your secret army. Although we might have to think about doing the shooting thing—'

'Well think about it very carefully. Because once you've joined the group there's no way back. Girls in the Soviet Union are also now fighting against the Nazi hordes; Dutch girls can do the same. What's more, they can operate more freely as they're less likely to arouse suspicion. No one expects innocent-looking young girls like you to get involved.' It was a reasonable point. Frans got up to leave. 'I'll be back in a couple of days to hear your decision.'

When their mother asked what Frans had wanted, Truus answered guardedly and not quite truthfully: 'He wants us to do things against the Germans that girls are good at doing because they are less conspicuous, so it means it'll be less dangerous.'

She didn't take a great deal of persuading. 'All right. Do anything against the Nazis that you feel is right. But be very careful and never let each other down, especially if things do get dangerous. I couldn't be without you.'

The girls joined Frans's resistance cell and soon afterwards he notified them that they would be 'put to the test'. They must prove they had the guts to carry out their assignments. A meeting place was arranged in the private woods behind a large colonnaded house.

Truus and Freddie turned up at the allotted time, apprehensive about what their new boss had in store for them. With a bit of luck they wouldn't be asked to kill anyone.

Suddenly Frans appeared out of nowhere, startling the pair, and told them to sit on a mouldy stone bench beside a pond. Then he casually asked them for the address of one of their contacts: a Jew with communist associations. But the girls knew only too well that you never gave out a person's address, not to anyone, it was too risky. Nonplussed, the sisters refused. Now Frans drew a gun, pointed it at them and cocked it. 'You've been fooled,' he snarled. 'I work for the Gestapo.' As proof he reached into his coat pocket and took out some documents covered in German writing and swastikas. 'Now give me that address.'

'You bastard!' cried Truus.

Frans aimed the gun menacingly at Freddie. 'Now!'

Truus demanded to see his papers again and in the brief moment that Frans looked away the girls leapt on him, hitting, punching, scratching. They wrestled him to the ground and kicked the gun away. Truus quickly grabbed it and held it to his temple while Freddie sat on top of him and smacked his head with one of her shoes.

'Stop!' yelled Frans. 'Stop! It was just a test!' His nose and lip were bleeding and an eye looked badly hurt. 'My orders were to see how reliable you are. The gun's not even loaded.' He groaned in pain.

'You're such a bastard!' Truus screamed again. Only then did the girls realise that they too had bruises, bleeding knees and ripped clothes. Without another word they proceeded to help each other off the ground and slowly limp their way out of the woods, heads held high.

They had passed the test. Truus and Freddie were now the only girls in the ten-strong resistance cell run by Frans van der Wiel.

The summer of 1942 saw the beginning of the deportations of Dutch Jews to the death camps, mainly Auschwitz and Sobibor. The Resistance intensified its efforts to rescue the Jews and Truus took on a number of perilous missions in which she escorted Jewish children to safe hiding places while sidestepping German troops, the Gestapo and Dutch collaborators.

The first such mission involved 10-year-old Rebecca, who had been given a false identity as 'Louise' and a 14-year-old boy using the name 'Frits'. Alone and without their families (presumably deported) they had been temporarily sheltered by sympathisers but needed more secure sanctuaries. Louise was shy and fearful. But Frits was a spirited adolescent who had grown restless and bored after weeks of being sheltered by an older couple who forbade him from going outdoors or making any noise. He had become too much of a handful.

Truus and the two youngsters pedalled off on their bicycles to the arranged destination of Hillegom, some 14 kilometres south of Haarlem. They were dangerously exposed on the main road, which had very few side roads to duck into in case of emergency, only the fields of hay where earlier in the year tulips had bloomed. So they were all jittery. But some hours later they arrived safely.

Truus delivered Frits to his new 'foster family'. They were farming people with land, greenhouses, barns and animals. The sturdy young boy would be given outdoor work to do and kept busy in the fresh air. And the farmer couple weren't bothered by his adolescent exuberance. 'I know what that's like!' the wife laughed. 'We have a teenage boy of our own.'

Frits would live there contentedly with them until the end of the war.

Louise was taken in by a childless couple who treated her well and grew to love her. When it became clear that her own parents had perished, she remained with them.

A later rescue mission would turn out very differently.

Following a tip-off from a decent Dutch policeman that a house in which a large number of Jewish children were being sheltered was earmarked for a police raid, the Resistance received an urgent appeal to find alternative addresses for them. Truus was tasked with escorting a group of twelve children by train to Dordrecht, about 100 kilometres to the south, in the guise of a German Red Cross nurse. A cover story had been devised to keep the authorities at bay: the children, aged between 3 and 14, were ostensibly stricken with a contagious ailment and destined for examination at a children's home. Truus had been supplied with an official travel permit and other necessary documents, all correctly signed and stamped.

The children arrived by ambulance at Amsterdam Central Station, where she met them wearing a nurse's uniform and a stern expression, clicking her heels and exclaiming '*Heil Hitler!*' at passing Nazi soldiers. Once aboard the train, she ordered the children to sit down in their compartment and keep quiet. She had been expecting two other Resistance members, one posing as a soldier and another as a second nurse, to accompany her on the journey, but the soldier had disappeared and the nurse never showed up. She worried that something had gone wrong; she would have only herself to rely on now.

As the train pulled out of the station Truus was overcome with fear. Sweating and trembling, she struggled to hold on to her well-rehearsed veneer of self-assurance. Feeling like an abandoned child herself, she was close to tears. But forcing herself to muster up some of her feigned courage, she turned to the children beside her and began quietly talking to them, explaining who she was and what was really going on. She put the youngest, 3-year-old Rosie, on her lap, so that the little girl could see out of the window.

Changing trains at Rotterdam, Truus played her role well, hustling the children along with shouts of '*Schnell, schnell!*' And if anyone came too close to her charges she would wave them aside with a brusque '*Gehen Sie weg!*' Go away!

They boarded the Dordrecht train and entered their compartment. But a moment later a German guard armed with a submachine gun slid open their door. Truus sprang to her feet and raised her right arm with a loud *Heil Hitler!* The guard was followed by a Nazi officer. Truus's heart pounded. Her performance would have to be faultless.

'*Aufstehen!*' she yelled at the children (stand up!). The shocked and scared group rose to their feet. Then she ordered them to follow her in enacting the complete Hitler salute. '*Heil Hitler!*' Hesitantly the children raised their arms and repeated the words. All except for the eldest child, a 14-year-old boy who remained seated, his face pale and eyes full of pent-up resentment. He wouldn't stand up and he wouldn't salute. Truus slapped him hard across the face and bellowed again, more loudly: *'Heil Hitler!'* His eyes welled up with tears. And he slowly lifted his arm and uttered the hated words.

The officer nodded his approval. Truus handed him her papers and after a cursory inspection he returned them with a polite bow, offered her a cigarette and lit it, then left the compartment. She dropped back into her seat, drained of emotion, hair damp with sweat beneath her nurse's cap. She gazed at the subdued children sitting around her. The 14-year-old, his cheek still crimson, looked back at her with an expression of sheer loathing.

In Dordrecht she left the children in a park near the railway station while she called on the contact who was to provide her with a map of her onward journey. It would be a hazardous one. They would have to crawl through a prearranged opening in a barbed wire fence, then cross a minefield in order to reach the Oude Maas River, where a flat-bottomed rowboat would be waiting for them. Their final destination was on the other side of the water. The map plotted a precise route avoiding the mines and Truus studied it very carefully.

After nightfall they set off. The flat terrain was periodically swept by searchlights, so they would have to keep very low and very quiet. They inched along the route in single file, on all fours, with Truus in the lead beside little Rosie, and the 14-year-old boy bringing up the rear. One wrong move could end in an almighty explosion.

Truus was so relieved when they had all crossed the minefield and reached the field beyond that she burst into sobs. The children gathered around her, scratched and sore from crawling on the rough ground. Everyone was tired and cold, as well as hungry because they hadn't eaten since morning. But now they had to wait a while longer before making for the boat; their crossing had to coincide with the river's most favourable tidal conditions. Truus had brought along a fluorescent watch in order to know when it was time to go.

The delay seemed endless, the children grew increasingly restive. But at last the time arrived. Silently they headed towards the boat a short distance away. Truus got into the cold water and held it steady as, one by one, they climbed in. Then she pushed the boat into deeper water and with a great effort pulled herself in. There were four oars and the older children at once began to row rapidly.

But the sound of the creaking oars carried over the barren landscape and in an instant the searchlights began scanning the area from all sides. As the lights fell squarely on the boat with its crowd of desperately rowing occupants, it seemed the game was up. What chance had they now of slipping away across the water to safety? The oldest boy, the one who had balked at doing the Hitler salute and been slapped for it, now stood up in the boat and cried out: 'Go on and shoot, you goddamned Nazis!'

A machine gun opened fire, bullets tore through his body and he fell overboard, upsetting the balance of the boat. It capsized and everyone else tumbled into the cold dark water, where the strong current pulled them away from each other. To the background noise of machine-gun fire, screams and crying, Truus tried to grab the nearest children but the water was flowing too fast. She managed to return to the riverbank, but on an impulse rushed back into the water in a last frantic attempt to save someone, anyone, although it seemed hopeless. And miraculously she caught a child by the arm, held fast and turned back towards the bank. It was Rosie. She was alive, choking on mouthfuls of water. All the others were lost, shot or drowned.

She grabbed the girl and crawled away into the darkness, as behind her a motorboat began chugging slowly along the Oude Maas, headlight gleaming on the water. With Rosie in her arms, Truus retraced their earlier steps until they emerged again on the other side of the barbed wire and reached the road. Exhausted, in shock and traumatised by the horror that had befallen the children for whom she had been responsible, she staggered to the nearest house and hammered on the door.

Here at least they were in luck. The couple living at that random house were not informers. Not only did they care for the two girls, both suffering ill effects from the night's ordeal, but the husband did his best to camouflage their trail from the meadow and even sprinkled pepper on the ground to put tracking dogs off their scent.

They stayed with the couple for a few days until they had recovered, then Rosie was taken to a refuge in Dordrecht and a despondent Truus made her way back to Haarlem. But her nightmares about the mission's tragic ending would go on, more or less, until the end of her life.

The resourceful Frans devised a special brand of resistance work for Truus and Freddie. When he first told them about it, they gaped in disbelief and protested indignantly: 'It won't work!'

The idea was simple, sly, and lethal. The teenage pair – normally unadorned and unassuming, like typical Dutch schoolgirls – were to doll themselves up in seductive manner, with alluring clothes, high heels, make-up and perfume, then plant themselves in a bar or café frequented by a specific enemy target (i.e. a dangerous Nazi or treacherous collaborator) and lure them away with a promise of hanky-panky. They would then lead them to the small private woods 'for some privacy', where Frans or another member of the cell would be lying in wait with a gun … and bang! No more bad guy.

'You're crazy!' said pint-sized, baby-faced Freddie, who still wore her hair in braids and looked about 12. 'Those men will be able to tell that I'm not a whore.'

Frans admitted that she had a point. After a moment's deliberation he altered the plan slightly. 'All right, Truus will be the seducer and you Freddie will act as lookout and warn us if anything goes wrong.'

On the day of her first 'Mata Hari mission' Truus stood before a mirror studying herself. Red lips, pungent perfume, heels that pinched her feet, slinky dress highlighting the ample breasts she hated but which would obviously now be an advantage.

'You're so beautiful,' sniggered Freddie.

'Shut up.'

Frans and the others laughed too and eventually Truus joined in. There was definitely a comical side to it all. Still, this was serious undercover business and she had to believe in the role she was playing.

The target was a German SS officer involved in intercepting secret SOE transmissions. The Resistance had learned that he possessed information regarding future British airdrops which could lead to the capture of Allied agents. Frans's group had been observing him, they knew which Haarlem restaurant he favoured, and that he blatantly liked girls. He had been pointed out to Truus from a distance: an unremarkable-looking man in his fifties wearing glasses and with medals on his uniform.

Truus and Freddie entered the restaurant with the 10-guilder note they had been given and sat down. The target wasn't there. But at a nearby table another German soldier was entertaining an attractive young Dutch woman who was tucking into an elaborate ice cream sundae. While waiting for their man, they decided to order the same.

The sisters from an impoverished family had never before enjoyed anything so delicious. After finishing their desserts they ordered two more.

Still the target hadn't arrived. Perhaps he wasn't coming at all that day. They decided to leave but when the waiter handed them their bill they saw with a shock that it came to nearly 14 guilders. Emptying their pockets they could only rustle up a few extra cents between them. Their faces burning from the unwanted attention they were now receiving from the other customers, they meekly apologised to the waiter.

'You dirty little sluts!' he yelled, before grabbing hold of them and hustling them out of the door. Humiliated, ashamed and not a little angry at Frans for coming up with the whole damned idea, they returned home.

But only two days later Truus and Freddie unexpectedly ran into the very man they were targeting, on the street not far from his favourite eatery. Truus wasn't in her seductive get-up this time, in fact she was looking quite ordinary. But she smiled at him coquettishly and that was clearly enough to pique his interest, which she found rather satisfying.

'Go away and play somewhere,' she said to Freddie in bossy older-sister manner, and Freddie understood that she had to hurry off and inform Frans that the game was on.

The SS man invited Truus to the restaurant, where they spent a leisurely hour or so. He sat back, drinking beer and smoking cigarettes and periodically leering at her full young breasts, while she sipped a soft drink as she chatted and flirted. She told him all about the private woods, only a few minutes' walk away – 'and so romantic!' – owned by 'her uncle'. He laughed approvingly, remarking with a sly smile that she probably wanted him to 'teach her a thing or two'. She blushed like a naughty schoolgirl. 'Well, let's go,' he said at last.

Outside she spotted her sister on the other side of the road; Freddie signalled her that all was ready and sped away on her bicycle.

Ambling down the street towards the woods, the German lost no time in demonstrating his sexual zeal, kissing her hard on the mouth, fondling her breasts and bottom. She wondered whether they would actually make it to the woods or whether he would just drag her behind the nearest bush. Unused to this activity, a disgusted Truus found it hard to feign enthusiasm. She was also nervous and afraid. But she would have to keep pretending.

They finally reached the grand colonnaded house with the garden and woods behind it, the place where Truus and Freddie – a long time ago, it now seemed – had passed their initial test. They strolled down the path leading to the pond. Halfway there they stopped for a steamy embrace.

A loud voice interrupted them. It was Frans. 'What are you doing here?' he demanded in German. 'What's the meaning of this, Kitty? You know this is private property. I will report you to the authorities if you don't leave at once.'

The embarrassed Nazi straightened himself, apologised and clicked his heels. He and Truus turned to walk away. Seconds later, from behind, Frans shot a single bullet into the officer's head and he collapsed.

She had been expecting this but even so, Truus felt sick with revulsion. Freddie and another cell member emerged from behind the foliage and began to remove the dead man's uniform and boots. Meanwhile, Truus vomited where she stood.

They dug a hole between some bushes, dropped the body into it and covered it up. Then they fled the scene, taking the German's uniform and gun.

That night the sisters sat with their arms around each other, crying and cursing a war that had compelled them to carry out such a horrible act. But Frans later reported that the notebook the SS man had been carrying contained a wealth of information of great value to both the Dutch Resistance and their contacts in London. So in the final analysis maybe all was indeed fair in love and war.

There were other, similar, operations. And as the war dragged on and the girls hardened themselves to the horrors, the suffering and the deaths, they undertook assassination missions on their own. Always on their bicycles – enabling them to leave a scene quickly – and carrying a gun 'to feel safe', they developed a technique for cycle-by shootings. By now they had been trained to use weapons, and Nazi torturers and Dutch collaborators who threatened the lives of Resistance members and Jews were all fair game. Their movements would be monitored, daily habits noted, and at the optimum moment, as they walked alone down a quiet street, Truus and Freddie would swiftly pedal past, pull out their pistols and fire at close range. On other occasions, Freddie would ride on the back of Truus's bike as they ambushed their prey. By the time people emerged from neighbouring buildings and a crowd of onlookers had gathered, they were gone. And no one would suspect the Dutch teenagers – especially petite Freddie with her braids, tiny hands and girlish voice – of being gun-toting executioners.

In 1943, Frans brought a new member into their close-knit resistance cell. Three years older than Truus, her name was Hannie Schaft. Initially annoyed that they were no longer the only girls in the group, Truus and Freddie gradually developed a close friendship with the attractive redhead and they would work together on a number of missions involving both sabotage and assassination. Not all were successful.

With her aura of quiet sophistication, Hannie – who until recently had been a law student, cultured and well-read – was a sharp contrast to the artless working-class Oversteegens. But they soon saw that she was just as dedicated an anti-Nazi as they were. After being forced to leave Amsterdam University for not signing the requisite oath of allegiance to the German occupiers, she became involved in low-level resistance activities in the capital. But she yearned to take part in more audacious acts involving weapons.

In one of their more spectacular jobs together, as part of a wider sabotage team, Truus and Hannie blew up the railway between Haarlem and IJmuiden, the port city used by the German navy to store its torpedo boats. As the group set off into the hushed moonlit night, Sten guns dangling from their shoulders, Hannie giggled, 'We look just like the Bosch.' After setting their explosives they waited in a hidden bunker for the distant grinding and creaking of the approaching train, glanced anxiously at each other as it came closer … then cheered at the thunderous explosion, the screeching of steel and the feel of the ground quaking around them. They toasted their success with bottles of wine. 'Now I feel like a real partisan,' a contented Hannie told her friend on the way home.

Sometimes while on an operation Truus and Hannie would disguise themselves as a young courting couple, with Truus wearing men's clothes, her hair stuffed inside a jaunty workman's cap, playing the part of boyfriend. It gave them a pretext for dawdling at some location where they had to carry out covert surveillance.

There was one operation that Truus, Freddie and Hannie refused point-blank to undertake. It might not have been proposed were Frans still in charge. But by the autumn of 1944 all Dutch resistance organisations were absorbed into the new Forces of the Interior, under the command of Prince Bernhard of the Dutch government-in-exile in London. Resistance groups were reshuffled and new leaders appointed, not all of them to the girls' liking.

One such was a man called Maarten, who announced one day that he had an important assignment for them. The Germans had been stepping up their arrests of Resistance members and throwing them into Amsterdam's brutal Weteringschans prison, where torture and almost certain death awaited them. Previous attempts to free these comrades had ended in disaster, so now he had come up with another plan. They would kidnap and threaten to kill the children of a certain high-ranking Nazi administrator. 'We'll force the bastard to make a choice,' Maarten declared. 'Set the prisoners free or have your children killed.'

'Oh how wonderful,' pronounced Freddie. 'Let's start using children in our fight.' She glared at Maarten. 'You can count me out! It's your plan, why don't you do it yourself?'

Truus put an arm around her sister. 'She's right. I'm sure as hell not going to shoot those kids if the plan fails.'

'And what about the prisoners?' shouted Maarten. 'Don't their lives matter to you?' He paced the room angrily. Then he turned to Hannie. 'How about you?'

'Well, I would welcome another plan,' she replied calmly. 'We would all love to liberate the prisoners but not that way. We're not Hitlerites, we're resistance fighters and we don't murder children.'

And that was the end of Maarten's big idea.

The three girls afterwards ruminated on what an easy time these commanders had, concocting their plans and then leaving them to be carried out by others, no matter how dubious the ethics involved.

Truus and Hannie's most famous double-act (infamous to the furious Nazis) was one they took on entirely on their own: the elimination of the Dutch traitor Ko Langendijk in March 1945. Before the war he had been a successful and fashionable men's hairdresser, but the occupation brought out the worst in this greedy, venal man. He became an informer for the *Sicherheitsdienst* or SD, the Germans' notorious security service, responsible for detecting and neutralising enemies of the Third Reich. In return for money, he would give them the names of Dutch citizens he suspected of being anti-Nazi. As a chatty barber he gained insights into his clients' sympathies and affiliations, whilst snipping and styling their hair. In due course he dedicated himself full time to the SD, strutting around pompously in his grey uniform.

The Resistance had already tried and failed to liquidate him on a number of occasions. Then one day Freddie rushed home to announce that she had just seen Langendijk walking in the city centre with his girlfriend. Truus and Hannie grabbed their 9mm FN pistols and leapt on to Truus's bike (Hannie's had a flat tyre, again) and they followed Freddie as she hurriedly cycled back to Haarlem's main shopping street. After a few minutes they spotted the traitor and his moll blithely strolling along, window-shopping. As Freddie rode off to check that there were no police or soldiers in the immediate vicinity, Truus, with Hannie perched on the back, slowly cycled some way behind the couple.

As they approached the Kruisstraat viaduct over the canal, Truus told Hannie to get ready. They had to get close to Langendijk – 2 or 3 metres, no more – in order not to miss. On the viaduct they waited until a small cluster of schoolchildren had walked past, then Truus gave the order to shoot. The bike wobbled a little as Truus took out her pistol from a pocket and steered with her left hand only. As they drew level with the traitor, both girls fired, Truus several times, Hannie's jamming as she tried for a second shot. Then Hannie raised her arm and managed to fire again. The SD man hit the ground, landing at the feet of his screaming lover. Truus and Hannie zoomed off as a crowd began to collect.

The whole operation had been so unexpected and taken place so quickly, they hadn't had time to work out an escape route in advance. And the police were already starting to arrive on their motorcycles with side-cars; the headquarters of the German police, the *Ordnungspolizei*, was only around the corner. The girls realised that soon the entire area would be sealed off as an investigation took place, with round-ups, house searches, the brutal grilling of witnesses, the terrible reprisals against innocent civilians. After all, the SD man was one of theirs.

Truus pedalled as fast as she could a few blocks north up the Kruisweg, until they were outside the Spoorzicht café. There they dismounted, Hannie removed her scarf and smartened her hair and an out-of-breath Truus removed the cap she always wore on missions to partly conceal her face. No sooner had they entered the café than the police turned up outside and began noisily to secure the square in front of the railway station.

They would have to pretend they had been in the café all the while, drinking. Truus knew the reputation of the barkeeper – he was a profiteer, not very trustworthy but he could be bribed. Allowing him a glimpse of her gun, she ordered two gins and said that when the police entered he was to tell them she and her friend had been in the café for an hour. 'I'll pay you well for it. But if you betray us you'll be the first to get a bullet.'

After a few minutes in the ladies' room, where the girls tarted themselves up with the makeup Hannie always carried with her, they returned and sat down on a banquette against the wall. At another table, a group of men were playing cards and Truus repeated her blunt message to them. Dumbfounded, they looked uneasily at her and at each other, but continued shuffling and dealing their cards. The barkeeper put the drinks down on the table in front of the girls, then sidled back behind the bar.

When two policemen barged in, Hannie and Truus subtly lowered their pistols beneath the table. They drank some of the gin before launching into a big show of sleazy drunkenness. The policemen demanded to see everyone's identity card and the girls groped around in their bags for theirs (needless to say they had long been using false identities). While Truus flirted crudely with one of the policemen, who pushed her away in disgust, the other questioned the barkeeper. He calmly shook his head; no one had entered in the past hour. Satisfied, the police left. Nervous tension relaxed at last, Truus collapsed into a heap.

Later they repeated the same boozy act in which they lurched up the street, laughing and singing. It got them through the police cordon. The grim-faced *Ordnungspolizei* officer was glad to see the back of them.

A few days after this triumphant operation, Hannie was stopped at a military checkpoint. A search of her bicycle pannier revealed an underground newspaper and her pistol. She was arrested. The vicious interrogations began, the beatings, a forlorn solitary confinement. They had long been searching for 'the girl with red hair' spotted at the scene of one of her assassinations. Aware of that description of her on the Nazis' most-wanted list, Hannie had been dying her hair black, but at the time of her capture her visible red roots gave her away. Witnesses were brought in and she was identified.

A desperate Truus tried everything in an effort to save her. To her fury the underground leaders seemed unwilling or unable to offer concrete help. In the end she blagged her way into Weteringschans prison in her old disguise as a Red Cross nurse, hoping to persuade the duty officer that Hannie was the girlfriend of a decorated German sailor, now languishing near death at the hospital where she worked. Would they allow the girl to be released for a short while – under escort, naturally – so that this loyal German patriot could say a final goodbye to her?

The officer sympathised with the story. Perhaps he even believed her. But it didn't matter because Hannie wasn't there. There were no longer any women prisoners at Weteringschans. 'You might find her at Amstelveenseweg prison in the south of the city,' he suggested.

At this second forbidding institution Hannie was made to sit in a waiting room with cowed souls hoping to get word of their incarcerated friends and loved ones. Each in turn was called into the office of a glowering female administrator. When Truus's turn came she explained politely that she was inquiring after Johanna, or Hannie, Schaft.

The woman turned the pages of a large book and ran a finger down the list of entries. She found Hannie's name, crossed out. '*Sie ist nicht mehr hier*,' she said matter-of-factly and snapped the book shut. No longer here.

On 17 April 1945 Hannie had been taken to the Bloemendaal sand dunes near Haarlem to be executed. It was later reported that when the first bullet only grazed her scalp she turned to her executioner and mocked him: 'I can shoot better than that.' Further shots ended her life and her body was dumped into a shallow grave in the sand.

Three weeks later the war was over. The remains of 422 members of the Resistance were eventually dug out from those sand dunes, 24-year-old Hannie, the girl with the red hair, was the only female among them.

Liberation should have been a joyous occasion for the long-suffering Dutch, especially after that final winter – the 'hunger winter' – in which the Germans did their best to starve the population of Holland and many in Haarlem were forced to eat tulip bulbs to survive. But with her cherished Hannie dead, Truus's spirit cracked and she suffered a nervous breakdown. In time she recovered and when she went on to marry one of her former Resistance comrades and have a daughter, she named her Hannie.

Chapter Five

Jacques Lusseyran –
When a Blind Boy Led the Sighted

As a young boy growing up in the heart of Paris, Jacques Lusseyran had an idyllic life with loving, kind and understanding parents. His father was a chemical engineer and his mother was a well-educated and highly intelligent woman. Carefree summer holidays were spent with grandparents in the Anjou countryside of western France. But this perfect existence came to an abrupt, traumatic end one day when Jacques was 8 and had a freak accident at school.

The boys were all piling out of the classroom for morning break, eager to get outside to the playground, when an older boy in a rush accidentally ran into him from behind. Being near-sighted, Jacques was wearing glasses, and as he was knocked off balance he fell against a desk and his right eye was pierced by one of the arms of his spectacles. The eye was damaged beyond recovery and had to be removed, and worse still, the severity of the blow had caused his injured left eye to lose all vision through 'sympathetic ophthalmia'. He was now totally and permanently blind.

In the weeks following the accident, once the initial pain had gone, Jacques began to develop different ways of 'seeing', sensing and relating to the outside world. He refused to feel sorry for himself and wouldn't allow anyone else to, either. Instead he discovered a kind of inner light which helped him to navigate his way through daily life, and while he no longer had vision in the conventional sense his internal world became magically bright and multicoloured: everything and everybody was imbued with its own distinct colour, visible only to him.

As time went on he developed an ability to move around on his own, both indoors and outside, by sensing the shape and proximity of objects around him with a kind of bat-like radar system; it is well known that all physical objects have their own electromagnetic fields and exude energy. Jacques realised that when he manoeuvred his way around with confidence he could get along fine, but when he was afraid of being hurt, then he truly was blind and at a loss. So he was soon back in the park and the playground, throwing himself into the old games and activities, with an occasional guiding hand from his friends.

He honed his sense of hearing to the extent that he learnt to interpret even the subtlest sounds around him, to distinguish between the slight variances in tone and resonance as sound bounced off the objects in any space. Everything had a voice which spoke to him; when a door gently creaked he could tell whether it was from a draught or a human hand. In particular he learnt to read the hidden meanings in people's voices. And every sound he heard, every object his fingers touched, and every taste and scent which entered his senses was transformed for him into the light and kaleidoscope of colour which he saw with his inner eye.

His parents had a major decision to make. Should they enrol Jacques in the highly regarded boarding school for the blind in Paris, or keep him living at home and attending the local school, scene of his terrible accident? After much deliberation they chose the latter course, for which Jacques would be forever grateful. His parents felt his blindness should not be treated as a disability that set him apart from others, but rather as a temporary setback, to be overcome by allowing him to engage fully with life and the world. In order to remain at his old school he would be required to read and write in Braille. This he learnt to do in six weeks. His parents acquired a rare Braille typewriter for him, which his mother also taught herself to use in order to supervise his homework.

He was given a Braille device to help him master the basic mathematical operations, but in the end he found he could dispense with it and do mental arithmetic instead. This sharpened his ability to memorise. He created an internal screen on which he could imprint figures or names or facts; a screen he could later visualise, conjured up from memory. This ability would prove immensely valuable to him a little later in his life.

Away from schoolwork, his boyish zeal for outdoor fun was undiminished. A 'jungle gym' was installed in his grandparents' garden, where he hurled himself around on ropes and rings, climbed ladders, turned somersaults on a trapeze and swung from parallel bars. And together with one of the local country boys he would charge through fields and farmyards, over hedges and into ditches ... both of them running as fast as they could, with Jacques held and guided by a shoulder, until they collapsed on the ground, muddy and scratched and laughing.

Jacques was growing into someone who felt in control of his destiny despite his blindness – in some ways perhaps even because of it – and he felt, if not invincible, then at least self-assured and unabashed.

When at the age of 10 he entered a prestigious central Paris lycée, he made a new friend called Jean Besnié and the pair soon became inseparable. Each morning Jean would call for him at the apartment house where he lived and they would walk to school together; in the afternoon Jean would accompany him home. They did their schoolwork together. They also spent hours chatting, exchanging ideas and observations on life. Jacques revealed to his friend his own special method of perceiving the world, without eyesight but using all his enhanced alternative faculties.

By their early teens the two boys were going on hiking excursions into the hills and forests outside Paris and on returning home Jean would exclaim to his family: 'It's amazing how many things Jacques made me see today!'

On 12 March 1938 a shocking world event crashed in on their happy existence: the *Anschluss*, Hitler's annexation of Austria. Jacques listened regularly to radio stations from different European countries and especially loved to hear German broadcasts. He was fascinated by the language and culture of Germany. But this shrill, aggressive noise blaring out from Radio Vienna – with a lot of shouting and *Heil*

Hitler-ing – startled him. He was only 13 but he grasped that the German language was being infected by ugly new thinking and that it signalled danger.

Over the coming months he spent some time every day studying German so that he could understand more fully what was happening in Germany and Austria and how it might affect the rest of Europe, and his own life.

When war broke out the following year Jacques and Jean spent a lot of time discussing its implications. On the one hand they were only adolescents and protected by their youth, so they could remain detached from it. But they kept asking each other: 'Is the war our business?' They both felt that inevitably it must be, sooner or later. At last Jacques announced his determination to 'wage war'. He didn't yet know how but he would make it his business one way or another.

France fell to the German invaders in June 1940 and Marshal Pétain signed his armistice with Hitler, instructing the French people to desist from all further resistance and embrace the new 'peace'. But the next day the little-known General Charles de Gaulle broadcast the opposite message on the BBC from London. He said the fight for France was not over and urged his compatriots to resist the Nazis in any way they could. This marked the birth of the French Resistance, and Jacques and Jean both heard the call.

That autumn, Paris under the Occupation seemed eerily quiet to Jacques. There were few cars on the roads, although he could always tell when German soldiers were driving by from the way their tyres screeched as they turned around corners. And on the Champs-Élysées and in the Place de la Concorde he could smell their presence from the type of cigarettes they smoked: sweeter than the French brands.

At his new school, the venerable Lycée Louis-le-Grand in the Latin Quarter, Jacques had a new history professor. Ardently anti-Nazi, he took the measure of the boys in his class and advised them to be careful of the views they expressed, for there were bound to be one or two classmates ready to inform the authorities should they hear anything counter to the new pro-German orthodoxy.

Meanwhile at home, his parents gave him sole use of two small rooms at the end of a long corridor, in the rear of their apartment on the Boulevard de Port-Royal. A bedroom plus a study whose walls were lined with his vast collection of Braille books, this became his private domain, his retreat. Here he studied hard for long hours, late into the night, and also received visitors. Many of his school friends sought him out: those who worried about the war and wanted his opinion. He always seemed the best informed among them and they looked up to him.

Jean still called for him each morning and as they made their way up the Rue Saint-Jacques, they would be joined by others converging on them from the side streets, eight or ten other boys all en route to the school. Sometimes they were solemn, sometimes they joked with each other – the only taboo was any talk of school. And Jacques always walked in the middle of the group, like a celebrity surrounded by his fan club. On arrival at the lycée, the concierge at the gate would call out with amusement: 'Well, well. It's the Lusseyran parade!'

By the spring of 1941 Jacques and his closest friends – Jean and now also two boys called Francois and Georges – decided they could no longer distinguish between the things which concerned them personally and those which concerned them in a broader sense, such as the state of the country and world events. From now on, it was all personal. He had urgent discussions with them at his private quarters at home and they agreed they would have to start a movement, an organisation. But what kind? And who should be asked to join? Would they need much money? Arms? And being blind, what sort of acts could Jacques himself undertake?

Within a few days there were ten boys around him, all wanting to join this new organisation and urging him on. He called them to a meeting the following week, when instead of the expected ten, fifty-two piled in. He explained that what they were starting was called a resistance movement and that as long as they were regarded as mere kids they would not fall under suspicion. They had to make the most of that. But in order to stay safe, from now on they couldn't meet in groups of more than three, they couldn't discuss their activities with anyone, not even their families or girlfriends, and there would be no childish cloak-and-dagger notions or, for the time being, talk of guns.

And just like that, aged 16, Jacques found himself at the head of a resistance movement.

A small central committee was formed and it was decided that Jacques would be in charge of recruitment. Naturally, their first task was to swell the ranks. Each potential recruit would be instructed to go and talk to Jacques at his 'domain' on the Boulevard de Port-Royal to be vetted. They wouldn't be given his name, he would be referred to merely as the blind boy. Only those who had been announced in advance would be allowed in, and only if they arrived within five minutes of the appointed time. These prospective members had to be trustworthy in every respect, because their organisation could not afford to be infiltrated by young traitors of the type the history professor had warned them about. With his keen intuition and almost psychic ability to judge character, Jacques would not be easily deceived.

Although he had long ago stopped being able to visualise faces, he could read voices better than anyone. He had learnt that even a person's most-guarded thoughts were discernible in the tones and rhythms of their voice. For example there was the occasion at school when his maths teacher entered the classroom and, as usual, clapped his hands and launched into his lesson. But Jacques noticed that on that day his voice, 'instead of falling into place at the end of a sentence as it should have done, dropping a tone or two down the scale, hung in the air ... as though the teacher wanted to hide something, put a brave face on it... .' Jacques listened closely. He was so familiar with his teacher's normal inflections and cadences that he knew something was wrong. The man was clearly unhappy. Soon afterwards school gossip revealed that his wife had just left him.

Jacques had another powerful tool to help with his recruitment drive: the phenomenal memory which enabled him to remember long lists of names, phone numbers and addresses, thus avoiding the risky business of writing such details down, even in Braille.

Over the coming months, a constant stream of boys made the journey to his quarters on the Boulevard de Port-Royal. Jacques would sit opposite his candidates, testing and probing them through a series of careful exchanges, 'plumbing their hearts', putting his intuition to work whilst sagely smoking a pipe in order to make himself appear older. He was looking for those with confidence, courage and commitment.

Six hundred were recruited: boys who expressed a desire to fight for France and democracy, freedom and honour, for traditional Christian values. And their movement was given a name: they were *Les Volontaires de la Liberté* – the Volunteers of Liberty.

Their prime mission was to provide the French public with accurate news of the war. The only newspapers being published in France at the time were Nazi-approved collaborationist organs, and fed on a daily diet of Nazi propaganda, most people were ignorant of the truth. The nightly BBC broadcasts from London of the Free French radio, which always began: *Ici Londres. Les Français parlent aux Français*, would have been a good alternative news source but they were jammed and often difficult to hear. In any case, listening to the BBC was strictly forbidden by the German authorities and many were too afraid to tune in.

The task of Jacques's movement would be to monitor news broadcasts from both the British and Swiss radio stations, gather and appraise it, then produce a news bulletin to be mimeographed in a couple of thousand copies and distributed amongst the populace, dropped through letterboxes and slipped under doors – initially in Paris, then beyond as well, as their network grew. But the operation would be about more than disseminating the news. Jacques saw it as a means of combatting apathy and defeatism, for already there were many in France who saw their future as hopeless. His movement would help maintain the fighting spirit of the French people until the inevitable, victorious return of the Allies to liberate them from the yoke of occupation.

And Jacques knew that his 'boy army' was ideal for the job. Firstly, unlike older men with wives and children to worry about and livelihoods to maintain, they had nothing to lose – except their own freedom, and possibly their lives if they were unlucky. Secondly, their youth gave them a good cover story. As youngsters they could move about freely and hang around, pretend to be playing games or loafing, socialising, looking harmless and innocent as they carried out their allotted tasks.

And the alarming report that several members of an earlier resistance group responsible for publishing underground papers had been captured and executed in French prisons, was insufficient to put them off.

Jacques's sympathetic and tolerant parents were aware of the kind of activity he had undertaken and gave him their support. They were risking a great deal by allowing their home to be used as the nerve centre for his movement. But it was decided that from now on, to minimise the danger to them, they should be told as little as possible. On the other hand Jacques did feel a need to confide in someone older who could advise him. The only other adult he knew he could trust completely and who would approve of what he was doing was his anti-Nazi history teacher. When Jacques and his closest fellow Resistance members approached him, he was eager to help and offered to meet them each week to discuss their concerns. This gave them all the encouragement they needed.

As the sale of paper and ink were controlled by the German authorities they had to be stolen, and reliable accomplices found with access to mimeograph machines. Jacques's oldest and dearest friend Jean was dispatched on errands around Paris, helping to sort out the logistics. At last, in October 1941, the Volunteers of Liberty began to put out their twice-weekly bulletins, conveying news on the progress of the war and denouncing Nazi atrocities: arrests, torture, the persecution of the Jews, executions, the suppression of freedoms of every sort.

Caution was of the essence. It wasn't just the German occupiers and their French collaborators they had to fear, but those fellow Frenchmen who were too frightened and intimidated to go anywhere near an underground movement and were made dangerous by their lack of discretion. Early on, one of their members fell prey to such a scenario. He had been distributing the news-sheet in the apartment building where he lived and spotted by a neighbour. Later, whilst out shopping, the neighbour remarked to a shopkeeper that he had no idea what was in the printed material the boy across the hall carried around but it was a risky activity and his father should put a stop to it. The boy was arrested and not seen again.

Up by five o'clock every morning, Jacques threw himself into his leading role in his resistance organisation. Throughout 1942 he committed to memory the 1,050 Paris telephone numbers needed for his work. At the same time he gave no less of himself to his academic studies and never went to bed before midnight. Only on Sundays would he allow himself some respite, when he and Jean took 25-kilometre hikes together in the countryside, arriving home at night dog-tired.

When winter came, the Parisians froze because the Germans shipped French coal to warm their own people back in the Reich, so there was little fuel left for them to burn. In his icy rooms, Jacques struggled to keep enough feeling in his cold fingers to be able to read Braille. But he carried on.

At this point contact was made with a young French journalist called Philippe Viannay, founder of a resistance movement called *Défense de la France* which printed and distributed an underground newspaper of the same name. The paper was bigger and produced in greater numbers than the Volunteers' modest news-sheet, they had a professionally equipped print room, branches dotted around Paris, cleverly disguised delivery vans, plus a radio transmitter and open channel to General de Gaulle's government-in-exile in London. In short, they had all the sophisticated means which Jacques's movement lacked. But they needed something Jacques could offer: a workforce of 600 boys ready and able to increase their paper's distribution tenfold. He and Philippe joined forces and proceeded to work out a complex system of clandestine communications between them. As a new member of the executive committee of *Défense de la France*, Jacques would be responsible for the distribution of its paper throughout France.

In February 1943 the paper had a vital piece of news to impart to the French public, one they would probably have missed otherwise: after several months of fierce fighting, the Wehrmacht had just been mightily defeated at Stalingrad. Surely this would mark a turning point in the war. The Red Army was on the offensive now and the blow to German morale was immense. The paper advised readers on ways they could assist the Allies through passive resistance.

Otherwise it was not a politically motivated paper. It adhered to no particular doctrine beyond the ideal of western democracy as embodied by Charles de Gaulle, Winston Churchill and Franklin Roosevelt, it was based on Christian morality and simple humanity. An attempt was made to coordinate their work with that of the organised communist resistance, which had its own underground publication, but the communists' struggle was strictly rooted in Marxist ideology and their guiding light was the Soviet Union. As far as they were concerned the *Défense* people were outsiders, so the approach was rebuffed.

Needless to say, all *Défense* articles were signed with pseudonyms; Philippe's was *Indomitus*: the indomitable. And every care was taken to protect the identities of all who worked for them. But they lived in daily expectation that something would go wrong somewhere; somebody would be betrayed. Their operation expanded day by day and the bigger it became the greater the risk of someone being caught. 'It's inevitable that we make mistakes,' Philippe told Jacques, 'each of us, at least once. So we must expect trouble.'

By early May they were printing the paper in 100,000 copies. Distributing such a large number around the country put a strain on their local members in the provinces, especially in the Nord region where their agents were getting overwhelmed. Jacques knew he had to appoint someone to go there as regional head and take control of distribution from Lille. Unfortunately the reliable and capable people in the movement who were well known to him were all occupied elsewhere, so he would have to entrust this role to someone new.

A 25-year-old medical student called Elio appeared at his apartment one day without prior arrangement, which was irregular. But he had been recommended by a recognised Resistance operative so Jacques felt inclined to give him a hearing. He was on the alert, however, feeling that something was not quite right. Elio's voice lacked a certain clarity, perhaps. And he was not assured by the man's handshake, which seemed rather heavy. Jacques's normal confidence in his instincts was somehow thrown off balance with regard to Elio and he couldn't quite settle on a 'yes' or a 'no'.

He decided to discuss the matter with his closest Resistance partner, Georges. Could they trust this man? There was much in his favour: he was well informed, had been involved in the Underground for the past year, and as a native of the Nord region was thoroughly familiar with it. He had offered to give up his studies and relocate to Lille immediately. How could they refuse? Still undecided, Jacques and Georges consulted Philippe himself, who carried out his own investigation into Elio. In the end Philippe felt they were being over cautious. So with some slight unease they recruited Elio, who left for Lille immediately and quickly got a grip of the Nord's distribution network, working effectively and for a while fulfilling their expectations.

On 14 July, Bastille Day, they put out a special edition of the paper in 250,000 copies – a record number – featuring articles written by everyone on the *Défense's* executive committee. Throughout the day, forty teams of ten members each, handed out copies of the paper to astonished passengers on the Paris Metro, as if it were peacetime and the most natural thing in the world. They had been armed with special 'tear gas pens' recently airdropped from London, objects which resembled ordinary pens but when pressed would release just enough tear gas to allow the user briefly to immobilise an adversary and, with luck, avoid capture. As if by a miracle the day progressed without mishap, there wasn't a single arrest. And no one had to use the pen.

Although Jean Besnié was not a member of the executive committee, he was nevertheless active in their movement, coordinating the activities of new recruits. He and Jacques still attended classes together, although by now they had graduated to the elite Upper First at the University of Paris. And he remained Jacques' constant confidant. Everyone in their movement experienced fear, on a daily basis, but Jean was the only one to talk openly about it to Jacques. That summer his fears grew and he had premonitions of imminent disaster. He even intimated that he could foresee his own death: 'When I'm gone, you mustn't think of me any more. But know that I will still be with you, although I can't explain how.' The words cut into Jacques. He too felt that they were standing on the edge of an abyss. They had been the best of friends since the age of 10 but the war had bonded them more closely, perhaps, than life in peacetime ever could have done. 'You will stay alive,' Jean told his friend. 'But I wasn't made for this life.' He sounded quite calm.

Early in the morning of 20 July 1943, Jacques was woken by his father's voice calling him: 'The German police are here for you.'

So it had finally happened. His arrest. 'Just a minute,' he answered. He jumped out of bed and as he put his clothes on with trembling hands, his thoughts raced ahead. The first thing he asked himself was: who denounced me? But his chief concern for now was that they shouldn't arrest the rest of his family. His parents would fear for him and want to protect him but they couldn't; it was he who would have to protect them.

Four armed soldiers and two SS officers had arrived to arrest a solitary blind student. They searched his room, scattering his Braille books all over the floor. But they weren't violent, and with Jacques playing the 'frightened little boy', one of the officers let him say goodbye to his parents before taking his arm and leading him in an avuncular manner out of the apartment, down the stairs and into a waiting car.

When they arrived at their destination, which Jacques assumed to be Gestapo headquarters, he was shunted from office to office by a posse of curious guards who kept asking him whether he was really 'the blind one'. His reputation, as they say, had proceeded him. 'Yes, I am the blind one,' he would reply, which obviously pleased them. And the truth was that for once he did feel utterly blind, because his apprehensions seemed to have diminished his other normally acute senses.

Then one of his interrogators reeled off the code names of fourteen leading *Défense* members, informing Jacques that they had all been arrested. He added: 'But where are Georges and Philippe? They are the only ones we are still looking for.'

It was a horrifying mass betrayal of their organisation. Thankfully Jean's name had not been mentioned. Was he still free? But if they knew about Jacques they surely had to know about Jean too. How should he play this?

(*Above*) The Podgorska sisters in Przemysl, Poland, in 1942. (*United States Holocaust Memorial Museum, courtesy of Dr Joseph and Stefania Burzminski*)

(*Below*) Stefania Podgorska at front middle, with sister Helena on her left and Krystyna Schillinger on right, back row: Max Diamant (Josef Burzminski) on far left with Krystyna's parents, after the war. (*Courtesy of Ed Burzminski*)

(*Above left*) Leibke Kaganowicz (on left) with fellow partisan Pietke in Orany, Lithuania, 1944. (*Courtesy of Saul Kahn*)

(*Above right*) Stephen Grady as a 14-year-old schoolboy. (*Courtesy of Stephen Grady*)

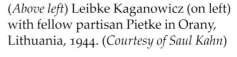

Truus and Freddie Oversteegen in Haarlem, Holland, in 1942. Freddie (top) is 17, Truus is 19. (*Noord-Hollands Archief*)

(*Above*) Truus Oversteegen (left) and Hannie Schaft shortly before one of their armed missions. Truus – dressed as a man so that they could pose as a courting couple – holds a bag containing Hannie's gun, while she puts on her gloves. (*Collection of the Dutch Resistance Museum © Harold van Welsenes*)

(*Right*) In this photo, having put on her gloves, Hannie has taken back the bag with her gun, while Truus reaches into her tobacco tin in order to roll a cigarette. (*National Hannie Schaft Foundation*)

(*Above*) Jacques's class at the Lycée Louis le Grand, 1941-42. Jacques is sitting in front, fourth from the right, and his best friend Jean Besnié is standing in the row behind, fourth from the left. (*Courtesy of Claire Lusseyran*)

(*Below left*) Jacques Lusseyran in Paris, 1946. (*Courtesy of Claire Lusseyran*)

(*Below right*) Hortense Daman in Leuven, early 1943. (*Courtesy of Mark Bles*)

(*Above left*) Hortense and Stephanie's homecoming in summer 1945. Hortense (right) is with her parents and nephew Michel. (*Courtesy of Mark Bles*)

(*Above right*) A 1944 self-portrait of Adolfo Kaminsky. (*Courtesy of Sarah Kaminsky*)

A corner of Adolfo Kaminsky's laboratory at 21 Rue Jacob, Paris, in 1944. (*Courtesy of Sarah Kaminsky*)

(*Above*) Edelweiss Pirates in Cologne, 1943/1944, with Jean Jülich on far right. (*NS-Dokumentationszentrum der Stadt Köln*)

(*Below left*) Edelweiss Pirates in Cologne, 1943/1944, with Barthel Schink, on far right. (*NS-Dokumentationszentrum der Stadt Köln*)

(*Below right*) Edelweiss Pirate Barthel Schink, about a year before his execution, with an Edelweiss flower on his jacket. (*Brandes & Apsel Verlag*)

The eight members of the Churchill Club in Aalborg after their arrest on 8 May 1942. From left: Knud, Jens, Mogens F., Eigil, Helge, Uffe, Mogens T., Børge. (*Museum of Danish Resistance*)

The members of the Churchill Club at the monastery in Aalborg on liberation, spring 1945. Knud Pedersen is standing on far right at the back, with pipe. (*Museum of Danish Resistance*)

Masha Bruskina's walk to the gallows with two fellow resistance members in Minsk, Belorussia, on Sunday, 26 October 1941. (*Yad Vashem archives*)

(*Above*) The *Rendezvous des Sages*, the wooden hut in the forest where Bouveret's fugitives would rest during their escape to Switzerland. (*Courtesy of Alain Nicod*)

(*Left*) Bernard Bouveret in 1943. (*Courtesy of Bernard Bouveret*)

(*Above left*) Helmuth Hübener in the middle, aged about 14, with best friends Rudi Wobbe (on left) and Karl-Heinz Schnibbe. (*Courtesy of Professor Alan Keele, Brigham Young University*)

(*Above right*) Helmuth Hübener in wartime Hamburg, about a year before his execution. (*German Resistance Memorial Center*)

Next he was taken to the office of an SS major, who told him without further ado that he had been condemned to death for subversion against the occupying authorities. They had proof that for several months he had been responsible for distributing all over the country the prohibited newspaper *Défense de la France*.

Strangely, Jacques refused to believe that he had received a death sentence, and told the major so. He expected a furious response but none came. Instead, after a pause, the major ordered his secretary to read aloud the entire fifty-page denunciation document compiled about Jacques, written in French. It was an account of all his Resistance activities, day by day, starting from 1 May 1943; every action he took in connection with his work for *Défense*. And his closest friends and associates in the movement appeared in the document alongside him, too many to count ... including Jean, who was described in meticulous detail.

He now knew without doubt that the traitor had to be Elio. The evidence contained in the document was a record of all that Elio had witnessed and heard since he joined the organisation on 1 May; the facts left out were the ones he had not been a party to. Philippe had been right: we all make at least one mistake. It was the only time Jacques had recruited someone in spite of his doubts and now their entire operation had been blown apart. How many would die because of it?

The initial questioning over, Jacques was taken to Fresnes Prison in the suburbs south of Paris, where the Germans incarcerated captured SOE agents and members of the Resistance. For the next six weeks he was brought back dozens of times to Gestapo HQ for further interrogation. Prisoners at Fresnes were routinely tortured but this was not the case with Jacques. He was beaten only once by one of his SS inquisitors, which caused him to shout angrily at the brute that he was a coward for thrashing a blind man who couldn't defend himself, at which the SS man merely laughed. But it didn't happen again.

His blindness seemed to give him a measure of protection. The Gestapo found it difficult to believe in the guilt of someone so physically restricted. Surely despite the evidence he must be essentially harmless. He must have been manipulated by someone else, higher up. They searched for but never found this elusive 'someone else'.

He was imprisoned at Fresnes for six months, part of the time in solitary confinement in a tiny cell, but he knew that all around him were others from the Underground, mostly men but women too, his soulmates in suffering. To know he was not alone was a comfort. At one point, during a prison medical examination, he crossed paths with his old school friend and fellow Resistance member Francois, who confirmed what he already knew: that Elio had been the traitor in their midst. Francois related the story of his own capture, engineered by Elio, who had met him off a train as he arrived back in Paris soon after the mass arrest. Under a pretext, he led Francois to a nearby bistro. After slyly handing him a pistol under the table, Elio snapped his fingers as though summoning a waiter, whereupon two Gestapo men appeared and arrested him. He was tortured; carrying a weapon was enough to ensure that, and when Jacques met him his body was thin and broken.

On another occasion one of his kinder gaolers brought Jacques a note from Jean. At last, long-awaited news of his friend! Jean told him he was being kept in another section of the prison, that he was all right and that he had high hopes for Jacques's future. He ended his note: 'I love you more than myself'. It was to be their last communication.

In January 1944 Jacques, together with some 2,000 other French prisoners, was transported by train to Buchenwald concentration camp near Weimar, in central Germany. In that hellish death camp he was reunited for a while with some of his fellow *Défense* comrades, before they were put into work commandos – entailing hard manual labour outdoors in all weathers – where life expectancy was short. After that he didn't meet them again.

In Buchenwald his blindness was both an advantage and a curse. The advantage was that he could avoid the work commandos. The curse, that he was quartered in the overcrowded, disease-ridden invalids' block, where the already meagre food ration was halved, and brutalised fellow prisoners would regularly steal what little bread and watery soup he was given. Starving and weakened, he developed an array of life-threatening illnesses – pleurisy, dysentery, erysipelas and ear infections – and was put into the camp infirmary, where people were not treated but merely laid down to either die or recover.

To the astonishment of everyone he slowly got better and the 'blind Frenchman' now achieved renown amongst his fellow inmates as 'the one who didn't die'. They stopped stealing his food. Instead they started seeking him out to confide in him and find a measure of hope. Jacques knew that once a person gave in to despair they died, so he saw his purpose as combating the 'infectious disease' of hopelessness and defeatism by keeping up his companions' morale. He reached deep into the resilient inner world he had forged out of his blindness to offer others his own formula for survival in the midst of suffering.

With his excellent German language skills, Jacques listened attentively to the German army's official news broadcasts, blasted out over the camp through loudspeakers. It was pure Nazi propaganda, of course. Even now as Germany was being beaten back on all fronts, they put a bullish spin on things. His job was to read between the lines and work out what it was they *weren't* saying. Then he would convey his interpretation of the news to the other inmates, block by block. Following D-Day he intuited the course of events as the Allies fought their way into France and by mid-August accurately figured out that the studiously avoided mention of any news regarding Paris could only mean that the Allies had reached the French capital and the Germans were on the verge of losing it. At last on 26 August he confidently announced to his fellow inmates that Paris must already have fallen. It had been liberated by the Allies the day before.

There would be another eight harrowing months for Jacques before his own liberation. In early April 1945, as General Patton's US Third Army neared, the SS forcibly evacuated most of the camp on a death march, leaving the rest of the prisoners to fend for themselves. Jacques was among those left behind. There was nothing at all to eat but they clung to life; by the morning of 11 April their hunger was so acute that Jacques and other emaciated prisoners chewed on the grass around the camp pathways.

That afternoon a 14-year-old Russian boy who had climbed on to the roof of one of blocks was first to spot the American flag on a Jeep as it pulled up at the gates of Buchenwald. For the survivors, the camp's liberation was their barely dreamt-of return to civilisation. Of the 2,000 French prisoners in Jacques's transport fifteen months earlier, he was one of only thirty still alive.

A week later Jacques had just gone to fetch some water for his block when a familiar voice called out his name. It was his old boss Philippe Viannay. The one who had got away. He embraced Jacques, who now learned that after their movement's betrayal Philippe had managed to evade capture and left Paris to join the Maquis, guerrilla-style resistance fighters, in the surrounding countryside. He had been shot several times. When Paris was liberated he made contact with General de Gaulle, who had now charged him with the task of repatriating liberated French deportees. And so he had come to Buchenwald to find his former *Défense de la France* members, if any had survived.

Jean, Francois, Georges and countless others were dead. But at Buchenwald Jacques and two other members were still alive. Philippe gathered the three of them together and led them to an official French car waiting at the gate. And so Jacques was driven back to Paris, to his old apartment and a reunion with the parents who had waited so long for him.

Chapter Six

Hortense Daman – A Grocery Delivery Girl With Fresh Eggs and Hand Grenades

The Daman family was central to the life of their community in the small Belgian town of Leuven, 25 kilometres east of Brussels. Stephanie Hortense ran the grocery store on Pleinstraat – a narrow street of terraced houses – which was a neighbourhood focal point, and her husband Jacques was a respected master shoemaker who worked at the Bata factory in Brussels. They had four children of whom the eldest, their son Francois, was a career soldier with the Belgian army as well as an accomplished athlete and equestrian. Their three daughters were Bertha, already married and with a child of her own, Hortense, and the youngest, Julia.

Opposite the corner house, which was both their store and family home, and across a square, was the guardhouse at the entrance to the big Philips electrical factory, an important local industry. Stephanie's grocery business regularly supplied lunches for the workers there.

The Damans' comfortable middle-class existence in this Flemish-speaking region of Belgium was dramatically altered by the onset of war. Francois was 26 when it broke out in 1939; Hortense, the sibling to whom he was closest, was half her age, at 13. Belgium had suffered horrendously from German aggression during the Great War and nobody really trusted them to honour Belgium's stated desire to remain neutral in this new one. So it came as little surprise when Germany invaded their homeland in its grand sweep of the Low Countries in May 1940. Francois immediately became active in the Belgian Resistance.

Along with millions of others from the Benelux countries and France, the Damans became refugees and headed west to escape the blitzkrieg, on those dangerous roads clogged with desperate fleeing families and prey to Stuka dive bombers. After two weeks' exhausting and demoralising travel on foot, they arrived in Lille on 29 May. But it was the end of the line. A German Panzer division had beaten them to it and an officer informed the Belgian refugees that their country had surrendered, the fighting there had stopped, and they had to return home. The Germans laid on trucks to return the Flemish-speakers to their homeland (they were considered culturally closer to the Germans and therefore more worthy), while the French-speaking Walloons were made to trudge back under guard.

When the weary Damans at last reached Leuven and their house, they were shocked to find it derelict, with the roof caved in (the result of artillery fire during the short-lived defence of the town), and looted of virtually every last item. It was a devastating sight. Equally alarmingly, they found that the Philips factory across the square, as a key manufacturing installation in the town, was now occupied by the German army. The earlier Belgian sentries in the guardhouse overlooking their home had been replaced by German soldiers. For the remainder of the war, the daily lives of the Damans would thus fall under the close scrutiny of the occupying authorities, which would have no small consequences for the hazardous activities in which they would soon engage.

For the next few months, while their home was being restored, the family moved into a small rented apartment in Brussels. The only good news was that Francois, a sergeant in the Belgian army, had survived the fighting and after a brief spell as a PoW had been allowed to return home. He now linked up with a number of the army's high-ranking, influential officers who together formed the clandestine Belgian Legion, which used the Red Cross as a cover for its resistance operations. The Legion had close connections with the British secret intelligence service MI6 and would soon come under the direct command of the Belgian government-in-exile in London.

As a trained mechanic and engineer, Francois could travel around the country without attracting suspicion. He now began to help some of the British servicemen, still at large in Belgium and France following the Dunkirk evacuation, to evade capture and be put on to the newly created escape lines southwards to Spain. The Comet Line, one of the most famous, was established by a young Belgian woman called Andrée de Jongh.

Although she had only just turned 14 and was too young to understand the intricacies of the war and the underground movements now ranging against the Nazis, the deeply patriotic Hortense was intrigued by what her brother was getting up to. She knew better than to ask too many questions, but was certain that he wasn't just doing work for the Red Cross. It was plain to Francois – as well as to their parents – that despite her tender age, Hortense was eager to help somehow. So he gave her a small initial task: to take copies of the illegal paper *La Libre Belgique* and leave them around for members of the public to pick up and read. She was thrilled to be asked.

'But be very careful,' he warned her. 'If you are caught the Germans will put you in prison.' He trusted his sister. She was intelligent and sensible. He would have preferred her not to get involved at all in resistance, but realised that her loathing of the occupiers and love for her country would make it hard for her to remain detached. Better that she should act under his supervision than get drawn by others into doing something foolish.

So she began occasionally to distribute the illegal paper, and when that was all going smoothly he approached her with another assignment. 'Will you take a letter to someone for me on the way to school tomorrow?'

'Oh yes!'

'Behave normally but keep your eyes open. Don't walk too fast, make sudden movements or draw attention to yourself in any way.'

Instinctively cautious, the next day she arrived at the rendezvous point early to check out the surrounds. She observed her contact arrive and sit down on the appointed park bench. When she was sure it was safe, she sauntered over and sat down beside him. She nonchalantly passed him the letter and he thanked her politely before calmly getting up and walking away. *Et voilà!* Couldn't have been easier. She had no idea what was in the letter. Only that it was important to Francois and his movement.

There were a few more letters and messages to be carried for him in Brussels. Then at last in October the family could move back into their home in Leuven. Stephanie reopened the grocery store but her business faced new challenges. Food was now in short supply and strictly rationed, so it wasn't easy providing the necessary provisions for her customers, who had to have ration books in order to buy. And because most of the petrol had been requisitioned by the Germans, deliveries could only be made by bicycle.

Francois had little choice but to give Hortense another task. As the Allied soldiers and airmen he was helping to escape obviously didn't have ration cards, providing them with enough to eat while on the run presented a real problem. But he had a plan for supplementing the available food supply. Again, his sister was eager to play her part. So after school she would cycle out to nearby farms and ask permission to pick up the pieces of beetroot and kohlrabi left over in the fields following the harvest. Sometimes she also persuaded the farmers to sell her bags of flour. As the unauthorised purchase and transportation of foodstuffs was banned by the German authorities, this meant Hortense was now officially a black marketeer, for which she could be imprisoned. The farmers warned her of German military patrols in the area, but Hortense was familiar with the hidden back routes leading to Leuven, and her forays remained undetected.

In the spring of 1941 Francois's underground contacts sent twenty fugitive British soldiers his way and he decided to shelter them in the attic of a convent in Leuven, aided and abetted by a few of its nuns. But how to deliver the food needed for so many extra mouths without anyone noticing? The convent was not far from Stephanie Daman's grocery store, so it was reasonable to expect that the nuns would buy food from her and that Hortense, who regularly delivered groceries for her mother after school, should cycle over with them. She just had to carry heavier loads than normal in her panniers – no easy thing over the town's cobbled roads – and visit more frequently. The Germans didn't notice the anomaly. For several weeks she helped feed the Brits – who were bored and claustrophobic in the convent attic, with mealtimes the high points of their day – until they were moved on and successfully made it back to England.

Besides delivering food to various safehouses and passing on messages for Francois, by the age of 15 Hortense was getting up early most mornings to buy food for her mother's store from Leuven's Old Market, which was controlled by German officials who had to authorise all purchases of produce. Her German was becoming fluent and she was also growing adept at using her 'innocent girlish charm' to win the Germans over. Soon they were smiling and calling her '*die kleine Hortensia*'. She never let her hatred for them show. That summer she left school for good.

Next, she began to smuggle copies of *La Libre Belgique* into the Philips factory. Francois brought them home and Hortense hid them inside her coat when she delivered the workers' lunches.

'*Guten morgen, Herr Kapitän*,' she would greet the captain of the guard as she passed the gate and entered the factory grounds.

'*Heil Hitler!*' he would dutifully respond.

The German soldiers on guard at the building's entrance waved her through as she smiled pleasantly at them. The sweet-faced blonde teenager with the lunch deliveries became such a familiar sight that they never thought to search her. Once inside, she waited until she couldn't be seen before sneaking into the men's locker room, where she left the copies of the forbidden paper. If their presence was reported to the authorities they wouldn't be connected to her because, after all, who would suspect a young girl of entering a men's locker room?

The first major blow to Francois and Hortense came in February 1942 with the arrest of Francois's close ally in the Resistance, Commandant Lambert – later executed along with many others with whom he had been working. Not only would the network have to be rebuilt, but Francois was himself now in danger of arrest, torture and execution, and could no longer operate in the open. He would have to go on the run, constantly moving from one secret location to another. Another fugitive without a ration book, forever looking over his shoulder.

Hortense was determined to continue her Resistance activities. But dodging the enemy no longer felt like a game.

That summer, Francois presented her with a tough new undertaking. As always, it would be risky and she would have to draw upon her cunning and initiative. He explained that she had to gain access to a scientist called Professor de Vleeschauwer, whom the Germans were keeping under house arrest. His politician brother Albert had escaped to London in 1940 and was part of the Belgian government-in-exile, as Minister for the Belgian Colonies. Albert had placed the production of all raw materials in the Belgian Congo at Britain's disposal in its fight against Germany. This was a considerable economic benefit to Churchill's government and didn't endear the de Vleeschauwer family to the Nazis. So they kept the professor – a potentially useful hostage – on a tight rein behind the high walls surrounding his house in Leuven, which was constantly patrolled by armed guards.

Albert de Vleeschauwer had sent a message from London to Francois's resistance cell, stating that he needed to make direct contact with his brother. This could only be done via a clandestine radio receiver. Naturally it would be impossible to smuggle a whole radio set into the house, far too big and obvious, but Hortense might be able to sneak in its separate components piecemeal, hidden beneath groceries … after first receiving permission from the German authorities to deliver groceries to this 'suspect' Belgian.

Hortense knew the first visit would be the trickiest. After all, no one at the professor's house had actually ordered any groceries and there was no way to alert him in advance. She would have to be allowed inside and somehow manage to speak to him alone, making him understand that she was not merely delivering vegetables but was a link to his brother in London.

She wheeled her bicycle up to the gates of the house and stopped before the two guards. 'What's this?' one of them demanded as he lifted up the cloth cover over her front pannier. Seeing vegetables and a small basket of eggs, he told Hortense to wait there while he took them into the kitchen.

'Please, I really ought to go in myself,' pleaded Hortense, 'as I've been instructed to do by my mother.'

Deprived of the opportunity to pilfer some of the goods on the way to the kitchen, the guard was understandably annoyed. 'All right,' he replied gruffly, 'but we'll go with you.'

The two guards accompanied her to the front door and hammered on it. It was opened by a maid who looked warily at the three of them. Francois had told her that the professor's household servants had probably been placed there by the Germans, so weren't to be trusted.

Hortense began to explain in a loud, loquacious manner that her mother's grocery business would henceforth be supplying vegetables to the professor and that she needed to speak to him to find out which vegetables he wished to order ... could she have a word with him so that she could go back and tell her mother ... etc. etc. ...

The maid still regarded her dubiously and Hortense was beginning to run out of steam when at last the bespectacled Professor de Vleeschauwer himself came to the door to see what was going on. She grabbed this one and only chance.

'May we speak privately, sir?'

He motioned for her to come inside. She moved with him as far indoors as possible and in a low voice explained the real purpose of her visit. Fortunately he was facing away from the maid and the guards, who were hovering in the doorway, so they couldn't see the astonished look on his face.

A moment later he was on board with the plan and evidently enjoying the cloak-and-dagger element. For the benefit of all ears present he thanked Hortense emphatically. 'I look forward to seeing you again,' he said. 'Stuck in the house with little to do, I'm taking more interest in food.' Then he told the maid to take the 'excellent vegetables' into the kitchen.

At each successive visit Hortense took with her a part of the radio, hidden under her vegetables, fruit and eggs. Valves and switches, resistors, wiring, all made it through. Luckily the soldiers guarding the professor's house quickly grew bored with the food delivery routine and after a cursory glance into her pannier, would let her in.

Hortense never knew what message Albert de Vleeschauwer was so eager to convey to his brother from London or why it was so important. She didn't ask such questions. But over and over again she willingly endangered herself – and her family – in order to enable him to convey it. Once again she successfully completed a difficult mission and impressed Francois with her resourcefulness. So at this point he formally recruited his 16-year-old sister into the Belgian Army of Partisans (BAP), which was supported by their government-in-exile in London, and of which Francois was the Intelligence and Liaison Officer.

She was to be a courier. It was a dangerous role in which she would constantly be moving from place to place carrying incriminating letters and parcels, but Francois felt she was more than capable of taking it on. Couriers in the BAP were generally girls because they were considered less likely than boys or men to be stopped and searched by the police and military authorities. They also had feminine guile on their side: a tool which could potentially disarm the intimidating men in uniform. But without doubt they also needed luck to survive. That was always the unpredictable factor.

Francois explained to her the structure of the organisation she was joining, in which a wide network of cells were grouped into different areas of Belgium, controlled by a central body in Brussels. Inter-cell orders and reports, vital information regarding attacks on German targets, messages about transporting weapons needed for an operation, intelligence about German army units which could prove useful for the Allies: this was the kind of communication Hortense would be carrying. 'The Nazis want to destroy our system of command and control,' he told her. 'And the best way of getting to the commanders is by identifying and arresting the couriers, who are the links between so many contacts within the BAP.' He warned her that if captured, the Gestapo would be merciless in their efforts to extract names and addresses from her.

'Just tell me what I have to do,' she replied.

'Your cover of delivering groceries for mother is perfect, providing a pretext for cycling to any part of Leuven, and your corps commandant will depend on you to keep open the lines of communication between all levels of command, from national to sector, corps and individual cells.'

From then on Hortense was very busy. Stephanie was now fully aware of the work her daughter was doing and the thought of what could happen to her if she were captured terrified her. She also knew, as did her husband Jacques, that it would have been futile to try to dissuade her. They just prayed that Francois could somehow protect her.

There was one thing, at least, from which Francois did manage to keep Hortense safe. The Resistance was full of red-blooded young men and he warned them all, in no uncertain terms, not to play around with his kid sister. Although she was self assured and evidently shrewd beyond her years in her role as a Resistance member, when it came to relations with the opposite sex, she was a total innocent. In that respect she was simply a typical, well brought-up Belgian girl of the times. And one who for the present was forced to relinquish a social life and the prospect of boyfriends – those would have to wait until after the war.

By 1943, Francois was more than ever involved in helping Allied airmen evade capture and enter the escape lines. Hortense assisted him in this role too. In one memorable mission, Francois and Hortense were tasked with moving two Canadian members of a downed Halifax bomber from one safehouse to another, on a dark wet night, after curfew. At one point, dangerously close to being discovered by sentries as they skirted around German military headquarters, Hortense pulled the airman she was escorting into a doorway and embraced him as if they were lovers. Fortunately the sentries – uncertain whether they had actually heard something through the rain or merely imagined it – decided not to investigate and get soaked, but stay under cover at their post.

Following their safe arrival at the new address, Hortense continued to smuggle in extra food for them. At well over 6ft tall the Canadians towered over most Belgians, which was problematic for when they required 'escape suits' for their onward journey to Spain. Stephanie managed to find some material on the black market and asked a tailor (a distant relation) to make two suits. When she gave him the outsize measurements, the horrified tailor exclaimed: 'For God's sake, don't tell me who they're for.' But he made the outfits and some time later, thus attired, the Canadians were ready to be moved on. The mission ended disastrously, however, as the resistance cell on which their fortunes depended had been infiltrated. The 'trusted contact' who picked them up by car for the drive to the French border turned out to be a collaborator, and the airmen were delivered instead into the hands of the Wehrmacht. They were sent to a PoW camp in Germany, to sit out the rest of the war.

There was always the danger of infiltration, of betrayal. For captured Allied crewmen, protected by the Geneva Convention and the generally more humane touch of the Wehrmacht and Luftwaffe, the result was a long spell of boredom in a Stalag. For the civilians who ran the escape routes it meant interrogation by the Gestapo and the SS, brutal torture, the hell of a concentration camp and/or execution. Hortense was involved in dozens of missions to help airmen, as well as escaped PoWs and slave labourers. Many succeeded.

In the summer of 1943 she discovered how easily calamity can strike, when she narrowly avoided it by virtue of being able to cycle faster than soldiers could shoot her.

She and another BAP member, Jommeke Vanderstappen, had been told to cycle to a nearby village to pick up a useful sack of explosives recovered from a bomb. When they got to the village they found the sack was heavier than expected, weighing some 40kg, but they hung it over the back shelf of Hortense's bicycle and fastened it down as well as they could. Then they set off back to Leuven and the safehouse where it was to be hidden, and where Francois was waiting for them.

Naturally the bike was now very heavy and not easy to manoeuvre. As she slowly and carefully rounded a street corner in the outskirts of town, she found herself facing a group of four soldiers on patrol, a little way ahead. Affecting nonchalance, she rode on by, ignoring the soldiers while desperately trying to control her weighed-down wheels on the cobbled road. Jommeke, as per the usual procedure, was cycling some distance behind. A moment later, as he paused at the same corner, he realised that one of the soldiers was staring at Hortense's bicycle, and at the road surface she had just cycled over. Glancing down himself, the reason became all too clear: the heavy sack had evidently torn slightly during the ride and now powdered explosive was leaking out onto the road. How could he not have noticed?

'*Halt!*' shouted a soldier, as he reached for the rifle hanging over his shoulder. The harsh, unexpected sound tore through Hortense. Looking back, she saw two of the soldiers running after her whilst the others raised their rifles to take aim. The next instant bullets ricocheted around her and she worked the pedals of her overweight bicycle for all she was worth, hurtling along the cobbles, heart pounding, leg muscles straining in agony, heading for the cover of the next street corner, some 30 metres away.

But behind the angry soldiers and unnoticed by them, was Jommeke, also taking aim. He quickly emptied his pistol at the soldiers, wounding one of them. Bewildered by shots from the opposite direction and fearing a large scale attack by 'terrorists', they dropped to the ground. Whereupon Jommeke leapt back on his bike and bolted.

Neither Francois nor Hortense dared tell their parents how close she had come to total disaster.

Shortly afterwards she had another terrifyingly close call. In preparation for an attack by the Partisans, she had been instructed to transport twenty-five hand grenades from one Leuven safehouse to another. They would be hidden in her front pannier beneath a layer of eggs, covered with the usual cheery red-and-white checked cloth. Once again the load made her bike heavy to ride and difficult to negotiate over the cobbles, and she struggled to keep her balance. But all went well until she found herself caught in one of the Germans' periodic 'razzias', in which a street was suddenly sealed off at both ends and everyone trapped there was subjected to a thorough search. The aim was to catch illegals: black marketeers, forced labour dodgers, anyone without proper identity papers.

Men were ordered to one side of the road, women and children to the other, and the searches began. Hortense cycled slowly to the kerb and put a foot on it to steady herself. She didn't dare dismount for fear of the bike toppling over and grenades spilling out everywhere. The discovery of the contents of her pannier would be tantamount to a death sentence. She had to think quickly. And this was when her innate genius for self-preservation kicked in. She knew she would have to use the most effective tools in her armoury: her tender age and her feminine charm.

She called out to a soldier who had begun searching the group of fearful women. 'Where is your officer?'

An unheard of act of insolence! He ordered her to shut up and remain with the others until her turn came to be searched. But instead she yelled past him to the lieutenant in charge, flattering him by raising his rank to captain: '*Herr Hauptmann, bitte!*' She asked permission to speak to him. His subordinate glared angrily at her but the lieutenant walked over.

'*Was ist los?*' he demanded. What's going on?

Hortense launched into a tale of girlish anxiety: she had been at the market for her mother but got delayed and now, with this further wait, she would be very late and in even worse trouble when she got home...

Impatiently, the lieutenant asked why she had been delayed in the first place.

Hortense lowered her eyes sheepishly.

'Well?'

She admitted shyly that she had been 'talking to someone'.

'Who?' The officer had an idea what the teenager was implying.

'A friend,' she replied.

'A boyfriend?'

Hortense nodded. The lieutenant's manner softened slightly and he nodded knowingly. '*Ach so ist das.*' But he was still duty-bound to search everyone. 'What have you in here?' He pointed to the pannier.

'Just eggs, *Herr Hauptmann*.' Being careful to hold the bicycle steady with one hand, she lifted a corner of the cloth to reveal the supply of wholesome brown eggs – a scarce and coveted commodity during the war.

'Have you authority for these?'

Hortense reached deftly into her pocket for the official authorisation papers she had received that morning at the market and handed them to the officer. He studied them and then, as he handed them back, she asked whether he would like a couple of eggs for himself.

'*Ja bitte*,' was the predictable response.

Hortense handed him two perfect eggs.

Realising he had compromised himself somewhat by accepting this gift, he was eager to see her off. 'All right, on your way now – hurry up!'

With a sweet smile and grateful nod, and taking great care to stay upright, she pushed off from the kerb and cycled slowly down the street until she was safely clear of the razzia area. Then she stopped and leant against a wall, shaking uncontrollably. The tension had been too much. Yes, she was artful and streetwise, invaluable traits in those perilous times. But she was still a young girl at heart and not immune to fright.

The Partisans stepped up their activities throughout 1943. There were attacks on railways, raids on fuel depots and warehouses, post offices were robbed for ration stamps and money, the crops of collaborationist Belgian farmers were destroyed, and traitors and informers were ambushed and frequently dispatched, along with members of the despised Belgian SS. And the more intense the activity, the more ardently the Gestapo and other security forces hunted down these enemies of the Reich.

By the autumn of that year Francois's activities both as a Partisan and an organiser in the Allied escape routes were well known to the *Geheime Feldpolizei*, the secret military police attached to the Wehrmacht. They also knew his real name and where the Daman family lived. They now mounted a surveillance operation on their house on Pleinstraat. The plan was to arrest Francois while on a visit to his parents. They just didn't know what the 30-year-old Resistance bigshot looked like.

Just before Christmas they seized a BAP member called Frans Vleugels, who before the war had been a professional soldier alongside Francois Daman. He turned out to be quite a catch. Some people required a great deal of torture before they cracked and gave up the information they were pressed for. Others, as we know, never cracked. They typically ended up dead. In the case of Frans, under torture he quickly told them everything he knew: the names of some 250 people active in the Resistance, together with their code names and addresses, the missions in which they had taken part, and the locations of the local safehouses they used. Hortense's name and role as BAP courier was included in the vast dossier the police compiled courtesy of Frans Vleugels. Within days the arrests began.

It would have been easy to pick up Hortense at this time but they were eager to catch the bigger fish as well – her brother Francois – so for the present they held off. They kept the Damans' home and grocery store under observation from the guardhouse of the Philips factory across the square, noting the comings and goings. Surely it was only a matter of time before he turned up. But Francois knew he was being hunted. He was already on the run, so had only to stay away from Pleinstraat and avoid detection. His family, on the other hand, were sitting ducks.

In the new year, to prove that despite the major setback to their organisation they could still put on an impressive show, the Partisans staged more actions: after ambushing and killing a patrol of Belgian SS men, they blew up the railway lines out of Leuven. The furious German authorities at last lost patience. They resolved to close the net on the Daman nexus.

On the cold, dark evening of 14 February 1944 – St Valentine's Day – trucks bearing soldiers and officers of the *Sicherheitsdienst* quietly surrounded the Damans' corner house. The family were sitting around their kitchen table, chatting and enjoying a simple, intimate supper together, their small dog sleeping in the warmth beside the fireplace.

In an instant their lives were shattered. Outside in the shadows a signal was given, at which both the front and rear doors to the house were smashed open and the heavy-booted men stormed in, shouting, overturning the furniture and striking the Damans with their rifles. They were threatened and beaten, and their property was thoroughly ransacked.

Then Hortense and her parents were dragged off to Belgian SS headquarters.

After a night alone in a dank and rat-infested cellar, Hortense was moved to Leuven's nineteenth-century Little Prison, an overflow facility from its Central Prison. The women's block was run by nuns, which was a mercy, as they sympathised with Hortense. They knew that she wasn't a coarse common criminal, like some of the other prisoners, and they didn't regard her – as the SS and Gestapo did – as a terrorist undeserving of pity. For the nuns she was a political prisoner who had acted out of conscience. When Stephanie Daman was also brought to the prison, the nuns – against the rules – allowed the two women to spend time together for mutual comfort and support. Stephanie too had been labelled a terrorist for feeding and sheltering Partisans and various escapees, and been as viciously beaten under interrogation as her daughter.

The verger of the prison chapel risked his own liberty by covertly allowing prisoners to send messages to their families on the outside. It wasn't long before Francois learned of the arrests. He was horrified and consumed with guilt for having involved his family in his activities. But he also realised there was nothing he could do. He couldn't risk the welfare of a large unit of Partisans in a precarious attempt to rescue his own kin. To compound his anguish, his imprisoned father – whom the SS knew was not implicated in any Resistance activity – was being held purely as a hostage, to force his son into the open. When that didn't work, Jacques was deported to Buchenwald.

Early each morning Hortense was taken from the prison to SS headquarters, where under constant threats and beatings, she was grilled about her brother and others in the BAP network. The interrogations went on into the small hours of the next day. Her knowledge of local partisan and resistance activities was extensive after her close involvement of recent years, but never did she consider divulging a single piece of information. She continued to claim ignorance of Francois's activities and his whereabouts, and scoffed at the idea that she been a secret courier, rather than simply her mother's grocery delivery girl.

An Allied bombing raid on Leuven in mid-May badly damaged the Little Prison and it was considered no longer secure. Along with a number of other women, Hortense was moved to St Gilles Prison in Brussels, a far harsher place, without the benefit of compassionate nuns or contact with her mother. It seemed the SS had now given up on Hortense, who clearly could not be persuaded to give up her secrets. The door to her new cell carried a sign: *Ter Dood Veroordeeld* – Condemned to Death.

Things changed after D-Day on 6 June. With Allied divisions now battling their way into France, the Germans started moving more prisoners from the occupied countries to concentration camps in Germany. In mid-June, 17-year-old Hortense was one of a large group of women transported eastwards, manacled to wooden seats on a four-day train journey without food or water. Their destination was the women's concentration camp of Ravensbrück, 77 kilometres north of Berlin. It was known as 'the women's inferno'. And indeed, that was where her real hell began.

In Ravensbrück, Hortense was among many prisoners to be subjected to barbarous medical experiments. In one of them the Nazi doctor applied a prolonged, super-high dose of radiation to her ovaries in order to sterilise her; the pain was excruciating. The order to find expedient methods of sterilising female undesirables — political prisoners, Gypsies, Jews, Aryan women who had had sex with Jews (race-defilers) and others — came directly from Reichsführer-SS Heinrich Himmler.

In another experiment, which made her extremely ill and almost proved fatal, she was given a massive dose of gangrene in her left thigh in order to study the after-effects and how she coped. Ever since

1942, when high-ranking SS officer (and Hitler favourite) Reinhard Heydrich died of gangrene from infected wounds sustained at his attempted assassination, the Nazis had been concerned with how gangrenous wounds ran their course when untreated, as the necessary sulpha drugs were not always available to wounded troops. They were curious as to whether amputation was always unavoidable.

Put into a ward for the most seriously ill and contagious prisoners, Hortense predictably contracted typhus, causing her hair to fall out. By now, severely malnourished, ill and with an untreated, infected leg, Hortense's chances of survival were minimal. But two months after her arrival in Ravensbrück she was joined there by her mother, shockingly gaunt and aged. Nevertheless her maternal presence bolstered the teenager's will to survive, they were both stronger when together.

Once again Hortense mustered up all her tenacity. After many weeks of lying in the infirmary she understood that if she didn't struggle back on to her feet and learn to walk on her damaged leg, the doctors would kill her off along with the other 'hopeless cases'. It was her final battle. Somehow she found the necessary strength.

Shortly before the Russians liberated Ravensbrück in late April 1945, in a last-ditch attempt to make a deal with the western Allies, Himmler allowed the Swedish Red Cross to rescue a number of concentration camp prisoners in danger of being killed by retreating SS guards, and transport them by truck to Denmark and Sweden. As a result 21,000 prisoners were saved from various German camps in what became known as the 'white buses mission'. Hortense and Stephanie were among those released from Ravensbrück.

In Sweden they were nursed back to health, then at the end of June they were repatriated to Belgium. As it turned out, the Damans were a lucky family. Hortense, now 18, her mother Stephanie, father Jacques and brother Francois all survived the endless horrors and hazards of the war and the family was whole again, safely back in Pleinstraat. This outcome was, in many ways, little short of miraculous.

Chapter Seven

Adolfo Kaminsky –
Boy Forger Extraordinaire

A dolfo's parents were Russian Jews who met in Paris in 1916, after they had emigrated there. Expelled as communist sympathisers a year later, following the Bolshevik takeover of Russia, they moved to Argentina, where Adolfo and his two brothers were born. The family acquired Argentine nationality (a fortuitous move, as it later turned out) but in 1930 when Adolfo was 5, they returned to France.

When the Second World War broke out they were living with Adolfo's maternal uncle in the small town of Vire in Normandy. For a while they had a protected existence under the auspices of Uncle Leon, a French national, Great War veteran and respected local market trader. At school, 13-year-old Adolfo and a classmate created a school newspaper. They raised funds to buy an old printing press, obtained a collection of discarded printing blocks and fonts and immersed themselves in the principles of typography, engraving and artwork printing. Unwittingly, Adolfo had begun to acquire technical skills he would call upon a few years later, when they were needed not for an innocent school paper but in the cause of a life-or-death struggle.

At 14 Adolfo left school behind and found a job at an aeroplane parts factory. But a few months later, in June 1940, the German army arrived, the Nazi authorities took over the factory and Jews were no longer permitted to work there. Its only two Jewish employees – Adolfo and his older brother Paul – were kicked out. With limited local work opportunities, the youngster responded to an advert for an apprentice clothes dyer in Vire, and was taken on.

His new employer was Monsieur Boussemard, a chemical engineer who taught him how to turn redundant khaki army uniforms from the Great War into navy blue or brown civilian clothes, to alleviate the worsening clothing shortage. Fascinated by the dyeing process and the effects of the different chemicals used, the precocious teenager began to experiment. He asked for some samples of dye to use on offcuts of the cloths his father, who worked from home as a tailor, had in his workshop. He asked endless questions of M. Boussemard, who in turn was pleased to pass on his knowledge of chemistry to his young apprentice. In particular, Adolfo was keen to master methods for removing stains from all types of materials. He realised that, with painstaking research and experimentation, you could find ways of removing every conceivable stain – even those made by so-called indelible inks. Before long, Adolfo had gained a wide reputation as the go-to expert who could eliminate even the most problematic and stubborn of stains – a valued skill at a time when new garments were either difficult to get hold of or unaffordable.

In the course of gaining this skill, his experimentation with chemicals caused a few disasters at home. His mother was livid when his dyes left a multicoloured mess on her pots and pans, and there were occasional explosions and the odd fire in the kitchen. But such mishaps were to be expected in the world of the eccentric inventor. After his parents banned further chemistry trials at home, Uncle Leon gave Adolfo the use of an empty property he owned, as his personal laboratory. *Formidable!*

At about this time Adolfo noticed something new in the window of a pharmacy in Vire, which he cycled past every day. It was a magnificent chemistry set, complete with test tubes, balloon-flasks, retorts and condensers – and to top it all, a serious-looking vertical microscope. For a few days Adolfo stopped at the window to gaze in wonder at the set he knew he could never afford on his modest wages. But eventually he went inside to inquire about it from the pharmacist, Monsieur Brancourt.

'What do you want to do with it?' he asked the boy.

'Chemistry experiments. I work at the dyer's and have already experimented with removing ink and other stains, now I wish to go further.'

M. Brancourt lifted the set out of the window display and showed it to Adolfo, demonstrating the different pieces of equipment. Then they discussed chemistry, about which the highly educated pharmacist knew a great deal. He took a liking to the inquisitive boy and agreed to reserve the set for him, allowing him to buy it piece by piece, as and when he had the money. And that was how the budding chemist gradually equipped his prized laboratory. M. Brancourt charged him only a fraction of the real cost of each component and as for the microscope, he threw that in for nothing.

Adolfo now scoured the town's second-hand bookshops and flea market for books on chemistry, devouring every volume he could find. Still that was not all. He began to make weekly visits to assist the chemist involved in butter production at the local creamery. The chemist had to measure the fat content of cream supplied by farmers, who might be tempted to cheat by diluting their cream with water. To produce high quality butter, a high fat content was important. The testing method was simple: some drops of the dye known as methylene blue were dissolved in a sample of cream, to see how long it took for the lactic acid to make the blue colour vanish. The longer it took, the less lactic acid, i.e. the less fat. Later in the war it would be this vital piece of information – that lactic acid nullifies certain dyes – which led to Adolfo's future career as a forger for the Resistance.

Before long the perils of Nazi occupation became all too plain to Adolfo's family. First the German military announced that it would be requisitioning Uncle Leon's spacious house to be used as an officers' brothel. This so incensed Leon that he kicked one visiting army officer down the stairs. Unsurprisingly this turned him into a wanted man and he was forced to flee Vire to avoid arrest. When Adolfo's mother (Leon's sister) wrote to him at his hideout in Paris, a friendly local policeman warned her that the letter had been intercepted.

She was now compelled to go to Paris herself and tell Leon the German authorities knew his address; he would have to flee once more. It was meant to be a quick trip to Paris and back. But she never made it home to Vire. Her body was found on the railway tracks. Had she fallen or was she pushed off the train during her journey back from the capital? Never satisfactorily explained, the death traumatised the Kaminskys.

Now lodging in reduced circumstances in the town, Adolfo found consolation in his passion for chemistry. Still employed at the dyeworks, he nevertheless made almost daily visits to the wise and kindly pharmacist, M. Brancourt, who entrusted him with fulfilling certain orders for customers. With the wartime shortage of most basic necessities, Adolfo used his private laboratory to produce bars of soap from bicarbonate of soda, and candles from paraffin and wax polish: homemade goods that became highly sought after in Vire.

It wasn't until the middle of 1942 that Adolfo realised Brancourt's pharmacy was a cover for his work in the Resistance, and that his mentor was involved in organising sabotage missions in Normandy. One evening Brancourt asked his young protégé: 'Would you be willing to make things for me that are more dangerous than bars of soap?'

The answer was an unequivocal yes.

Brancourt showed him how to produce toxic substances that corroded railway parts and transmission lines: a useful tactic for disrupting German transportation and communication systems. At last Adolfo felt he was doing something to avenge his mother's death. At 16, he had entered the Resistance.

A year later, Adolfo and his family were arrested as part of the general round-up of France's Jewish population, destined for the notorious Drancy internment camp outside Paris. By then most people realised that the brutalist concrete housing blocks were only a temporary holding centre ahead of transportation to Auschwitz and other death camps. In the packed cattle cars heading for Drancy, Adolfo's brother Paul acted quickly. He knew that as citizens of Argentina, a neutral country, the Kaminskys were entitled to its protection. Begging for pen and paper from the other prisoners, he wrote out several identical letters to the Argentine consul, requesting urgent help. He handed the letters to railway workers and anyone else within reach, throwing some out of the window, in the desperate hope that someone would bother to post at least one of them.

Interned at overcrowded Drancy, the family awaited its fate. The conditions were inhumane. They watched as groups of forlorn Jewish men, women and children arrived, suffered, and after days or weeks were taken away again to the trains, soon to meet their tragic end. But the Kaminskys lingered on, seemingly forgotten.

At last, after three months they received wonderful news. One of Paul's letters to the consul had mercifully got through to him and they were to be released; very few people were ever released from Drancy. As returning to Vire was no longer an option they would be penniless and homeless in Paris, but free.

Their discharge from Drancy came at the eleventh hour. Within a matter of days Germany suspended the diplomatic agreement to exempt Argentine Jews from deportation. In order to avoid imminent re-arrest, Adolfo's father hastily called upon an old contact now associated with the Resistance to help them acquire false identities and documentation.

When Adolfo, acting as go-between, met with a young member of the resistance group – codenamed Penguin – to discuss the details, he was advised to assume an official occupation as student.

'That's impossible,' said Adolfo. 'I need to work to earn my living.'

'Do you have a trade?' asked Penguin.

'Yes, I'm a clothes dyer.'

His contact raised an eyebrow. 'A dyer, you say?'

'That's right.'

'So you know how to remove ink stains?'

'That's my speciality,' Adolfo replied, his voice tinged with pride.

'And what about indelible inks?'

'No such thing. Any ink can be removed.'

Penguin explained that the document forgers in his group had a problem with Waterman's blue ink. 'It's been impossible to remove it. Do you know what we need to do?'

'Well, I'd have to analyse it to see what it's composed of.'

'I already know that – it's methylene blue.'

'In that case the answer is simple. You need to apply lactic acid.'

Penguin looked unconvinced. 'Are you sure?'

Adolfo told him about his work for the chemist at the creamery, the many chemistry books he had pored over, his home laboratory and endless experiments on stains, his production of soap and candles for the customers of Vire …

At the end of it all Penguin had one question: 'Would you be interested in working for us?'

A couple of days later he met with Penguin again to collect the forged documents for his family. The Kaminskys would be splitting up, some members placed on farms in the countryside – it was safer that way. As for Adolfo, from now on he would be known as Julien Keller and for the time being take a room at a young men's hostel in Paris run by the Salvation Army.

Through Penguin he soon met more of his new comrades: 'Giraffe', 'Heron', 'Otter'. These young men in their twenties, as Adolfo learned, had been members of the *Eclaireurs Israelites de France* (EIF), the French Jewish scouting movement, and continued to use their former EIF monikers as code names. After the Vichy government dissolved the EIF in 1941, many of its older members joined the French Resistance, forming their own units.

When the deportations began in Paris many Jewish children – including babies and toddlers – had been unavoidably left behind following the abrupt round-up of their parents. Some were alone in apartments, others wandered the streets. EIF members, often in hiding themselves, mounted stealthy night-time rescue operations, scooping up these abandoned children and hiding them in safehouses, convents, Catholic boarding schools and orphanages until liberation. They saved thousands.

The EIF group which Adolfo joined, responsible for forging documents, was known as *la Sixième*, the Sixth. It operated clandestinely within the official *Union Générale des Israélites de France* (UGIF) – General Union of French Jews – established by the Vichy government in order to contain and control the country's Jews in compliance with Nazi plans for their deportation. Upon realising that their organisation was in effect an instrument of Nazi rule and complicit in the deportations, a number of UGIF officials set up and financed the Sixth – composed primarily of the intrepid young scouts – to rescue as many as they could. These UGIF 'double agents' knew in advance which Jews were due for imminent round-up and notified the Sixth, which would urgently forge the official documents needed to allow those named on the lists to disappear under false identities.

Adolfo was the youngest of the group of five working at their laboratory in a cramped attic room, which was disguised as an artists' studio, complete with traditional skylight, at 17 Rue des Saints-Pères on the Left Bank. (The address was a secret from everyone else – not even their leaders in the Resistance knew where it was.) Two tables held their typewriters, blotting paper and other equipment, with hidden drawers underneath for drying documents. They dashed off some arty daubings to hang around the room, behind which they concealed their forged papers until required. And as part of the sub-terfuge, the inks and chemicals used for their forgeries sat on shelves alongside paintbrushes, turps and paints; the smell of chemicals didn't arouse suspicion in an artists' studio. So convincing was their cover that whenever the concierge or electricity-meter reader made an unexpected appearance, the 'artists' would be congratulated on their delightful paintings. They had to stop themselves from laughing, until the visitor had gone.

Adolfo, who had been experimenting with chemistry since the age of 14 and had years of training as a dyer, vastly improved the forging methods the group had been using before his arrival. With increasing cooperation between the different branches of the French Resistance, orders for their work poured in from a variety of sources besides the UGIF, even from the intelligence services in London. The workload was punishingly heavy: they produced hundreds of forged documents each week.

But the teenager didn't spend all his time cooped up in the attic lab, generating life-saving documents. His role also involved taking stashes of the blank identity cards he had produced – together with ink, pen, rubber stamp and stapler – to the homes of Jewish families destined for arrest the following dawn. Their passport-sized photos would be stapled to the cards, which he then carefully filled in, in the typical handwriting of a municipal pen-pusher, followed by the official stamp.

Even then, at that late hour and despite dire warnings, there were some people who refused the help on offer, dismissing the evil about to close in on them. Believing they would be protected by their indisputable 'Frenchness', they rejected the very idea of assuming a false identity. For Adolfo, who knew what awaited them at Drancy and beyond, this caused great distress. But there was nothing more he could do.

Travelling around occupied Paris with an attaché case full of blank identity cards, rubber stamp etc., was a perilous activity. If stopped and searched, he would unquestionably be arrested as a Resistance operative, tortured for information, then sent to a concentration camp or shot. On one occasion, in January 1944, he came heart-stoppingly close to it. He was sitting on the Metro, taking a short journey eastwards from Saint-Germaine-des-Prés to Père Lachaise, when he heard loud voices and footsteps – the unmistakable sound of an approaching *Milice* patrol making its way down the train. This political paramilitary organisation, kitted out in blue uniform and beret, had been founded by the Vichy regime to root out Jews and Resistance members. They were considered even more dangerous than the Gestapo and SS because as native Frenchmen they were familiar with their fellow citizens' regional dialects and had extensive knowledge of societal norms and customs, both rural and urban – all useful in catching out fugitives. 'Identity check!' they called out to passengers as they entered Adolfo's Metro carriage. 'Have all bags ready to be searched!'

Adolfo tried hard to mask his fear. But sweat began to appear on his forehead and his heart was thumping hard. With a militiaman guarding each door there was no chance of exiting unseen; they were slowly advancing towards him, scrutinising identity cards, inspecting bags and cases. Trying to appear calm and confident, Adolfo stood up and proffered his identity card to one of the militiamen, indicating that he had to get off at the next stop.

'Julien Keller, 17, dyer, born in Ain…' the man took it and read out the details in an imperious manner, studying the document with hard suspicious eyes beneath his blue beret. 'Keller – is that an Alsatian name?' he asked, referring to its German connotation.

'Yes.'

He grunted. 'All right. Papers in order.'

Adolfo knew full well his papers were in order – he'd made them himself.

Then he heard the dreaded question. 'What have you got in there?' The militiaman indicated Adolfo's attaché case.

A wave of panic swept through him. For a moment he felt the urge to run, but he knew that was impossible.

'Well, are you deaf? What's in there?' The militiaman was impatient now.

'My sandwiches.' Adolfo opened the attaché case and showed it to him. There were indeed some sandwiches inside, on top of the incriminating contents. Then 'Julien Keller' gave the man an adolescent's foolish smile. Adolfo knew that playing stupid and immature was his best shield. He'd cultivated the façade so that he could call upon it whenever necessary.

After a critical stare, he was waved away: 'You can go.' The doors opened at Père Lachaise station and Adolfo stepped out.

He was aware that the authorities were scouring the city for the elusive 'Paris forger', the criminal mastermind who was supplying the Underground with a vast quantity of counterfeit documents. But they were naturally looking for an older man with a professionally equipped printer's workshop and paper mill at his disposal. Not an ingenious boy with a deceptively gormless expression, who was making it up as he went along.

In March 1944, he was summoned to meet a leading resistance figure known by his *nom de guerre* of Cachoud. This was Maurice

Loebenberg, the professional engraver who headed the Sixth and also played a major role in the *Mouvements Unis de la Résistance* (MUR), a body which united different resistance movements. He was based in Nice, where he had earned a reputation as a first-class forger of identity cards, birth certificates, baptism certificates, marriage certificates and food ration cards for Jews in hiding, deserters, Resistance members and Maquis fighters.

'I've heard a lot about your skills,' he told Adolfo. 'Do you know how to replicate watermarks? Relief stamps? Remove the ink on documents without affecting the colour of the paper? Make new paper look old?'

He answered yes to everything, reckoning that even if he didn't yet know *quite* how to do all those things, he would simply experiment until he found a way.

Cachoud was pleased with the self-assured teenager. 'As you can do everything, would you be able to set up a photoengraving studio? Our photoengraver in Paris, who has been doing good work for us, has said he is stopping because he's afraid his workers are getting suspicious of him. We need someone to take on this important job.'

After a short training course from the uneasy photoengraver and studying books on the subject purchased at the bouquinistes' stalls along the Seine embankment, Adolfo – claiming to be an amateur photographer – set up his studio in a spare room allotted to him at his boarding house on the Rue Jacob. He got down to work.

Photoengraving was a valuable tool in the forgery business, used to make printing plates for reproducing graphics of all kinds: lettering, line drawings, watermarks, etc. It was at 21 Rue Jacob that, working alone, Adolfo discovered techniques which enabled the Sixth to create wholly new documents indistinguishable from genuine ones, so that they no longer had to falsify originals. He converted paper to make it thicker or finer, to match the types made for different documents by the official state printers, and made copies of the official rubber stamps. It was easier to start from scratch than to remove the big red 'J' – which was a death sentence – from a Jew's identity card, without changing the paper's colour and texture.

His equipment was cobbled together from odds and ends gathered at junk shops, and he continued to invent. To create the centrifugal force needed to cover photographic plates with photosensitive fluid, he used a spinning bicycle wheel; to make paper appear aged he created a machine from which dust and ground pencil lead could be transferred on to it via a cranking handle; and inspired by Leonardo da Vinci he devised a gadget using a mirror and lenses to project an image of a design which had to be replicated by hand, making it easier to draw precise lines.

Adolfo and his comrades in the Sixth were always always hard at their work but their most challenging order came that spring when an anxious Penguin informed him that in three days' time the Nazis would be launching a round up of Jewish children staying at ten children's homes across Paris.

'How many children are involved?'

'300.'

Three hundred children, each requiring three documents – birth and baptism certificates and a ration card – added up to 900 documents. In three days! A seemingly insurmountable task.

He and the others set to their labours: making and ageing the paper, trimming it to size, typing and writing by hand, colouring, stapling, stamping. They slaved away doggedly, afraid to voice the fear that they couldn't complete the mission on time. At night, when the others went home, Adolfo carried on without respite, weary and weak from hunger, eyesight faltering from the painstaking, intricate work. More than anything he was terrified of making some small technical mistake due to a momentary lapse of concentration. The documents had to be perfect. Lives depended on it. He fought to stop himself from nodding off. He couldn't afford to sleep. He was able to produce thirty blank documents per hour. If he slept for one hour, he told himself, thirty children would die.

After toiling for two days and two nights, on the morning of third day they could at last glimpse the finish line. Reeking of chemicals and dripping with sweat, they egged each other on by counting out loud as they completed each document: 810 … 811 … 812 …

All of a sudden Adolfo was unable to see or hear anything and his body went numb. Overcome with fatigue he blacked out and fell to the floor. When he came round the others urged him to stop his work but he insisted on resting for no longer than an hour. There were still more documents to complete.

Through sheer willpower and self-belief they got the job done in the allotted time and the 300 children could be spirited away before the dawn raids took place.

The boss of the Sixth, Maurice Loebenberg (alias Cachoud) relocated from Nice to Paris in May, with the important new job of combining forgery operations in the south and north of the country under the recently created *Mouvement de Libération Nationale* (MLN), the National Liberation Movement. From then on he and Adolfo had many dealings together, with the demanding Cachoud keeping his young forger extra-ordinaire on his toes.

One day in early summer, Adolfo met with a contact in the Zionist youth movement, the *Mouvement de la Jeunesse Sioniste*, who had an urgent matter to discuss with him. He was liaising with an intelligence agent from London called Charles Porel, who had supplied weapons to his group and promised to deliver more. But Porel was keen to know the extent of the Jewish resistance network and how many potential combatants they could produce. 'I'm to draw up a list of names for him,' said the contact, 'including the people working at your lab, and its address.'

'Are you mad?' Adolfo retorted. 'I'm not giving you any names or addresses. How do you know you can trust this man Porel? It could be a trap.'

'We've looked into him and it's all safe. Cachoud trusts him.'

But Adolfo remained wary and refused to cooperate.

'You're just a coward, afraid to fight,' spat his contact before storming off.

On his way back to the lab he wondered whether he'd been right. Surely if his boss, the prudent Cachoud, trusted this agent from London it had to be a bona fide connection. And yet...

His fellow forgers of the Sixth agreed that the secrecy of their lab took precedence over all else and they shouldn't get involved with this man Porel and his promised supply of weapons to Jewish fighters, even at the cost of being labelled cowards.

In the following weeks an exhausted Adolfo grew uneasy, even paranoid. Was he being watched, followed? That man in the doorway … the couple sitting on a bench … the shifty-looking passer-by … were they spying on him? He slept badly, was underfed and his eyesight was giving him trouble. But there was no time to see a doctor. So he carried on, hoping that liberation would come soon. The Allies were drawing ever nearer to Paris. How much longer could it take?

Then in late July came the horrifying news which somehow perhaps he had feared all along. At a gathering of leaders of the Zionist youth movement and other affiliated armed resistance movements, organised by the 'agent from London' called Charles Porel, the Gestapo had swooped in and arrested the lot. It had been a set-up. As it later turned out, Porel was in reality a ruthless German agent named Karl Rehbein. Cachoud was seized in the same operation and tortured to death, his body dumped in woods outside Paris; he was 28 years old. The others arrested with him ended up on trains to death camps in the Reich.

For Adolfo's final major assignment at the secret lab, Penguin asked him to produce the necessary documents for a group of thirty Jewish children he was due shortly to escort to safety. Working overnight, Adolfo completed the papers and delivered them to his grateful comrade.

Three days later an ashen-faced Otter appeared in the lab and announced that Penguin and the children had been captured. Penguin – real name Marc Hamon – was only a few years older than Adolfo, but as his recruiter into the Sixth he'd had a protective, almost paternal attitude towards him and his loss was a great blow. He and his young charges were sent to Auschwitz, never to return. How excruciating that these innocents had got to within a whisper of surviving the war. Only a week or two later Paris was liberated.

The war was not yet over, however, and Adolfo still had a task to fulfil. Impressed by his outstanding accomplishments as a forger, the newly reconstituted French army's secret intelligence service decided it could use him too. They needed someone to create documents for their agents, who would be sent behind enemy lines to locate and investigate conditions at the concentration camps before the Nazis had time to dismantle them. This posed a new challenge for Adolfo, as he had not yet forged German documents. Now an official 'state forger' for France with greater funds at his disposal, he put together an extensive, well-equipped laboratory and print room, where he developed the techniques for producing German passports, ID cards, travel permits and even train tickets, cinema tickets, library cards, sales receipts, medical prescriptions and so on, in order to construct an entire fabricated back story for each undercover agent, calculated to pull the wool thoroughly over the Third Reich's eyes.

And he was thus kept usefully occupied until the Nazis capitulated and the war was won.

Chapter Eight

The Edelweiss Pirates –
Rebels with a Cause, and Guitars

In Germany, the Nazi regime's grip on the lives of its citizens was near total. And just as important as control of the adult population was indoctrination of the young. Children were carefully supervised, so as to be moulded into loyal followers of the Nazi Party creed. As Adolf Hitler declared in a 1933 speech about Nazi education policy: 'I want a brutal, domineering, fearless, cruel youth. There must be nothing weak or gentle about it. The splendid beast of prey must once again flash from its eyes. That is how I will create the New Order.'

Between the ages of 10 and 14, boys were enrolled in the *Deutsches Jungvolk*, and from 14 to 18, in the Hitler Youth, where they would be trained as future leaders of the Third Reich and indoctrinated in Nazi ideology. Girls were considered less important than boys and were to be prepared primarily for marriage and motherhood through membership of the *Bund Deutsche Mädel*, or League of German Girls. All other youth organisations, such as the Scouts, were banned.

In the early years following Hitler's ascent to power, the Hitler Youth was a tempting prospect for a teenage boy. There were leisure and sporting activities, races and competitions, camping trips with sing-songs by the campfire – all providing the sense of unity and comradeship enjoyed by young males. There were summer camps which were very popular, as they gave kids the opportunity of a holiday – for the poorer boys, these were the first real holidays of their lives, and for many city dwellers, their first experience of the countryside.

But by the late 1930s, as Germany headed towards war, the organisation became more militaristic and a blatant recruiting and training ground for future soldiers. In 1939, membership of the Hitler Youth became compulsory for teenage boys (except the Jewish ones, who were naturally excluded), and by the following year it reached its maximum size: with 8 million members, it was the largest youth movement the world had ever seen. It was a criminal offence for any group of youngsters to meet socially or for any other reason, except under the direct control of the Hitler Youth or League of German Girls.

However, there will always be those young people who reject the brainwashing, who balk at regimentation and won't be corralled into officially approved groupings. That was where the Edelweiss Pirates came in. They were gangs of working-class boys – and girls, too – who had left school at 14 to work in the factories and mills of Germany's industrial heartland, the region of the Rhine and Ruhr valleys. Some younger kids, still at school, also attached themselves to the Pirates. Eschewing the approved tidy and obedient look, they had a nonconformist air about them, the boys with their longer hair, colourful checked shirts, short dark trousers, thick white socks and neckerchiefs, maybe a leather jacket.

Unlike the offspring of the professional middle classes, brought up to respect and defer to authority, these sons and daughters of the labouring classes came from families with socialist/communist sympathies, trade unionists much given to striking in the early 1930s (before Hitler banned the unions in 1933) and mistrustful of the state. As such, they were naturally inclined to kick against authority of any kind.

In different towns the gangs went under different names: in Essen there was the *Farhtenstenze* group, translating roughly as Roving Dudes; in the cities of Oberhausen and Dusseldorf there were the *Kittelbach Piraten*; and Cologne was home to the biggest and ultimately best known, the *Navajos*, named after the Native American tribe known for its skilful combat techniques against the early colonists. But although they maintained separate identities based on their different locations, the gangs all belonged to the widespread network of Edelweiss Pirates and wore its symbol – the white alpine edelweiss flower which represented for them a pure, innocent kind of German patriotism – in the form of a small metal badge, usually hidden beneath a lapel. There were estimated to be more than 5,000 of these 'misfits', with 3,000 in Cologne alone.

Many of them owned a guitar or another instrument and enjoyed making their own musical entertainment. Where the Hitler Youth sang their militaristic marching songs, glorifying fighting and dying for the Fatherland, the Edelweiss youths played popular American jazz numbers, forbidden by the Nazis as 'degenerate' music, and songs by banned Jewish composers. They even wrote their own proud little ditties, such as:

> *We march by banks of Ruhr and Rhine*
> *And smash the Hitler Youth in twain.*
> *Our song is freedom, love and life,*
> *We're the Pirates of the Edelweiss.*

At first they were happy merely to flout the Nazis' restrictions on free movement, getting together in cafés or parks, hiking or riding their bicycles into the countryside on their own private camping excursions. There in the woods and glades, away from the prying eyes of the Nazi Party, they had the space and freedom to be themselves. They also travelled to other towns to meet up with fellow Pirate groups. But these were all illegal activities and, if discovered, could result in unpleasant consequences: an arrest, a beating, certainly a head-shaving: a common method of ritual humiliation. Equally prohibited was the intermingling of boys and girls so brazenly enjoyed by the Pirates. The government-approved youth organisations kept the sexes strictly segregated, all the better to regulate their adolescent emotions and hormones.

One of the girls who joined the Navajos in Cologne was Gertrud Koch, nicknamed 'Mucki'. Her father was a boilermaker and mother a pharmacist. The family were no followers of the Nazi creed; for eighteen months in 1938–39 they hid and looked after a Jewish musician in their allotment garden. There would be no membership for her of the *Bund Deutsche Mädel*, that alliance of Hitler-adoring girls suited primarily for breeding 'racially pure' babies for the Reich —

some of whom went so far as to send love letters to the Führer, offering to have *his* baby. Whenever he appeared in public, they were there in the crowd, identical in their dark blue skirts, white blouses and black neckerchiefs, hair in tidy plaits, screaming and swooning and weeping with ecstasy (just like the girls of a later generation would at a Beatles concert). All utterly risible in Mucki's eyes. Naturally, she fitted right in with the free-spirited Navajos.

All Edelweiss Pirates were sworn enemies of the Hitler Youth, whom they regarded as uniformed brutes and lackeys of the Nazi Party. Whenever a group of Pirates chanced upon a Hitler Youth street patrol (these were junior enforcers who abused Jews, stole with impunity and generally terrorised the neighbourhood), instead of running away they would stand their ground and fight. They tended to win these battles, perhaps because as working-class lads they were used to a rougher street life and fending for themselves. They were also not averse to carrying knives (tucked into their socks) and later on, stolen pistols. In any case, at least one Gestapo officer is recorded as demanding the police 'ensure that this riff-raff is dealt with once and for all, because the Hitler Youth are taking their lives into their hands when they go out on the streets'.

Undeterred, the Pirates of Cologne would converge in the woods and hills, get out their guitars and sing:

> *Hitler's power may lay us low*
> *And keep us locked in chains,*
> *But we will smash the chains one day,*
> *We'll be free again*
> *We've got fists and we can fight*
> *We've got knives and we'll get them out*
> *We want freedom, don't we boys?*
> *We're the fighting Navajos!*

The idea of teenage boys with knives might resonate uncomfortably in twenty-first century Britain, with its crisis of drug- and gang-related knife attacks. But in the Germany of the Nazi era, when the regime was itself the equivalent of a ruthless criminal organisation, the Edelweiss boys would have regarded carrying a weapon as a sensible measure – especially as their Hitler Youth foes, upon passing a 'courage test', were issued with a fancy dagger of their own.

After the war began, the Pirates' activities grew both more serious and more daring. No longer was it enough to organise clandestine outings to a rural retreat, sing banned songs, sport their jaunty anti-authority clothes and hairstyles, and bash a few Hitler Youth boys. They now endeavoured, wherever and however they could, to hinder, frustrate and slow down the Nazi war effort.

It started with spray-painting slogans on public walls, such as *Down with Hitler!* and *Down with Nazi brutality!* 'However often these inscriptions are removed,' a Nazi Party official in Dusseldorf complained to the Gestapo, 'within a few days new ones appear on the walls again.' Then the Pirates began putting anti-Nazi propaganda material through people's letterboxes, including Allied leaflets dropped from RAF planes. This was already regarded as treason, punishable at least by imprisonment in a concentration camp.

Walter Mayer was one of the Dusseldorf Pirates. The 16-year-old would get together with fellow members at a local café and play pool. Typically, one of them would ask 'What are we going to do next?' and another might reply 'Well, you know the Hitler Youth store their equipment in the big school shed, right? Let's make it disappear.' 'Okay, when should we do it?' A time would be agreed. And so they would raid the unguarded equipment store, to the wrath of their teenaged Nazi adversaries. Besides stealing their gear, the Pirates took to deflating the tyres on their bicycles. And when the novelty of that caper wore off, they would snatch the bicycles themselves. Enraged complaints against the Edelweiss renegades mounted up.

Meanwhile in Cologne, one of the most avid Edelweiss Pirates was a boy called Jean Jülich. He had already suffered in his brief life, owing to Nazi brutality. Born in 1929 in a working-class area of the city, he was just 7 years old when he saw his father, a waiter and member of the Communist Party, being dragged out of his home and badly beaten by the Gestapo. He was convicted of treason and sentenced to ten years' hard labour. With his mother out all day working in an umbrella factory, Jean was sent to live with his grandparents.

At 13 he was placed in a railway workers' training centre, where he began training as a machinist. The place was imbued with the Nazi ethos. Jean hated the constant Hitler saluting: on reporting to work each morning there would be the mandatory *Heil Hitler!* If he wanted to go off and use the bathroom, it required another *Heil Hitler!* to the adult in charge, followed by a second *Heil Hitler!* on his return. All day long his hand would have to shoot up and down. Madness. So in 1942, now 14 and unwilling to accept any more forced indoctrination, he dropped out and sought companionship with the like-minded youths of the Navajos, with whom he played pranks on the Nazis. A favourite boyish trick was to pour sugar water into the petrol tanks of officials' cars, causing the engines to stall. But as the war progressed, they engaged in ever more dangerous acts against the regime. Based in a deserted bomb-disposal bunker, the Navajos began to supply black market food to forced labourers and Jews on the run, concentration camp escapees and German army deserters, and to shelter these fugitives from the authorities.

With adolescent showmanship they derailed ammunition trains and threw bricks through the glass roof of a munitions factory in order to sabotage the machinery below. They grew ever more audacious, linking up with organised resistance units to raid army camps for arms and explosives with which to attack Nazi targets. Not surprisingly, the authorities reacted with increasingly repressive measures. Unlucky Pirates were rounded up and jailed or sent to reform school, forced labour camp, psychiatric hospital or concentration camp. They were regarded as juvenile delinquents, hooligans and outlaws. But being under the age of 18, they were too young to be conscripted and sent to fight at the Front.

Jean's friend and ally, Fritz Theilen, was a leading member of the Navajos. Like the majority of German schoolboys he'd been enrolled at the age of 10 in the *Deutsches Jungvolk*, but the authorities found him impossible to mould into a stereotypical Nazi boy and in 1940, aged 13, he was expelled for waywardness. On leaving school a year later he went to work at the Ford car factory beside the Rhine River in Cologne as an apprentice toolmaker. Witnessing the cruel treatment of the factory's slave labourers turned him even more strongly against the regime. Seeking the company of others who shared his opposition to Nazi ideology, before long he joined the Edelweiss Pirates and launched enthusiastically into their disruptive actions.

It was at Ford that he first dabbled in a little night-time sabotage. Together with an equally rebellious workmate, he would prise open boxes of spare car parts which had been stacked beside the embankment, awaiting transport to the Eastern Front, and fling them into the river. Carburettors, headlamps, ignition coils, whole engines – all sank to the bottom. When discovered, the crimes were blamed on the factory's Russian PoW slave workers and a group of them were rounded up by the Gestapo and shipped off somewhere, never to be seen again. No one suspected a pair of juvenile renegades.

In another ruse, they broke the tops off milk bottles and wedged the glass pieces into the tyres of vehicles lined up on the factory lot. As they were driven off the tyres burst with a loud *psssht* and went flat. After that the factory administration was on its guard. When the boys turned up early one morning in order to repeat the exercise they were seen by Nazi foremen, caught and thrashed. They had no glass in their pockets so nothing could be proven, but it didn't end well for Fritz's mate who, two years older than him, was already 18 and eligible for conscription. He was flung into the army and Fritz heard no more from him.

From 1942 onwards, Cologne was a frequent target of Allied bombing. Gradually the city was being bombed into rubble and its long-suffering citizens grew war-weary and disillusioned. This was not what they had signed up for a decade earlier when, in a burst of nationalist pride and optimism, they had voted Adolf Hitler into power.

Mucki [Gertrud] Koch's father was killed in a concentration camp in 1942, her mother lost her job and they had to leave their home. Money was very tight. Gertrud had hoped to train as a Montessori kindergarten teacher but the kindergarten was closed by the Nazis, Montessori principles being contrary to Nazi ones. At the end of that year she was arrested for her activities as an Edelweiss Pirate and spent several months in a Gestapo jail, where she was repeatedly beaten and had her arm broken when she was thrown down a flight of stairs. On her release the following May, the 18-year-old and her mother fled Cologne for a farm in southern Germany.

One day in 1943 Fritz Theilen was caught painting anti-Nazi slogans on a wall. Arrested and taken to Gestapo headquarters in Cologne, for several weeks he was viciously beaten and ill-treated. When at last he was released, the Gestapo no doubt reckoned he had been sufficiently terrorised into submission. But they were wrong. Far from abandoning his activities, Fritz launched into them even more wholeheartedly. No longer a factory worker, he lived rough with his Pirate comrades in the war-ravaged city's deserted, ruined buildings, and together they stole and looted in order to survive. In their secret lairs these outlaws listened to forbidden radio broadcasts from the BBC and spread news of the war, they continued to join forces with and aid escaped PoWs, forced labourers and Jews, and they attacked local Nazi officials. Any of these acts could have resulted in a death sentence.

By now many of these young boys – and the equally bold and courageous girls who united with them – had lost their fathers in the war, while others had parents imprisoned in concentration camps for political reasons. They felt isolated, with few friends outside their Edelweiss community, and many had been bombed out of their homes, which all added to their bitterness and determination to subvert the Nazi war effort. Perhaps their courage was partly due to a sense that they had little left to lose.

Further north in Dusseldorf, Walter Mayer was caught taking shoes from a bombed-out store, arrested and imprisoned. Eventually he was deported to a forced labour camp in north-east Germany, where he was put to back-breaking work in a stone quarry. Within a few months the harsh conditions and brutal treatment he received there led to him contracting tuberculosis. Weak and ailing, no longer of use as a worker, he knew this meant he would be killed off, so he decided to try to escape.

Under cover of heavy fog, he managed to flee the camp and reach a farmhouse a few kilometres away. It was always a risk, knocking on a stranger's door to seek help. Would he find assistance or betrayal?

This time the 17-year-old was in luck. The sympathetic farmer who opened the door took him in, and the next day, dressing him in his absent son's army uniform – a crafty disguise – he helped Walter board a train home to Dusseldorf. The end of the war was nearing and he was taken into hospital, where he eventually recovered.

It seemed the Pirates were not so easily contained by barbed wire and watch towers.

Fritz too had a lucky escape. Re-arrested in a Gestapo raid on a Pirates' hideout in 1944, he was moved from one prison to another until he ended up in a sub-camp of the infamous Dachau near Munich. But one night he managed to slip away unseen. He spent the last months of the war lying low, his Pirate days over.

This was how he avoided the terrible fate of several of his fellow Navajos. In the autumn of 1944, under the leadership of a 23-year-old concentration camp runaway called Hans Steinbruck, a small group of them had planned to blow up Gestapo HQ in Cologne, using detonators extracted from unexploded British bombs. But the plan was discovered and as they attempted to evade capture, Steinbruck and his co-conspirators shot and killed five Nazis. Before long the plotters were all rounded up and thrown into prison. On a smaller scale and with younger participants, the plot was nevertheless an echo of the army officers' conspiracy to assassinate Hitler with a bomb a few months earlier.

This time the repercussions would be severe. No longer mere infuriating rebels and delinquents, they were now seen as dangerous criminals and murderers. Reichsführer-SS Heinrich Himmler, Hitler's second-in-command and ultimate head of the Gestapo, determined to make a very public example of them.

Jean Jülich was one of several Navajos to be arrested for his alleged involvement in the bomb plot. Still only 15, he was locked in a tiny prison cell and taken out only to be interrogated and beaten. He was aware that in neighbouring cells his friends were receiving the same treatment. Then one day he noticed the others were being taken away.

There would be no trial, only summary execution. In the cold grey morning of 10 November 1944, in front of a suburban Cologne railway station and large crowd of curious bystanders, thirteen people were hanged on Himmler's orders. They included Steinbruck, of course, as the ringleader, six of his adult followers and six teenaged Edelweiss Pirates of the Navajo group who had been swept into his orbit and his plot. The three youngest to be executed – Johann Muller, Gunther Schwarz and Barthel Schink – were only 16 years old. Barthel, the son of a post office worker, had been an avowed opponent of the Nazi regime ever since, many years earlier, he had witnessed a Jewish barber being beaten by Brownshirt thugs. He had been actively involved in aiding Jews; now he had lost the fight.

As for Jean, he was transferred to a concentration camp where he survived a few more months of beatings, starvation and disease, until it was liberated by the Americans in the spring of 1945.

The lives of these young people would have been much easier had they kowtowed to the Nazi authorities, played by the rules and kept their rebellious nature in check. They knew all too well the risks they were taking by resisting, by fighting against the dogma they detested and the horrific war Hitler had unleashed. But the truth was that, just as the Nazis had an ideology, they had one too. And they believed in it strongly enough for it to spur them into action and sustain them through adversity. At its heart was a yearning for liberty and independence, and a sense of loyalty: to their friends, to those in need of their help and to the symbol of the edelweiss. They knew it was not they who were criminal, but the architects of the Third Reich.

For those Pirates who paid the highest price by forfeiting their lives, their ideals enabled them to meet the end with a quiet dignity astounding in anyone so young.

Chapter Nine

The Churchill Club –
Pipe-smoking Saboteurs

Knud Pedersen, a pupil at the posh private Cathedral School in the northern Danish city of Aalborg and the son of a Lutheran reverend, was appalled by the alacrity with which neutral Denmark had allowed itself to be occupied by Germany on 9 April 1940. Unlike neighbouring Norway, which battled on gamely for two months, the Danes capitulated within two hours. Of course, Danish military forces were woefully inferior to the mighty Nazi war machine and didn't stand a chance; the swift surrender saved many lives and avoided the possible bombing of Copenhagen. Nonetheless, Knud decided that if the adults refused to take on the German occupiers, he would do so himself.

The tall, lanky 15-year-old joined together with his brother Jens, a year older, and a small group of like-minded schoolmates, to launch a campaign of disruption and sabotage against the occupation forces based in Aalborg, in emulation of the Norwegian Resistance they admired. They called themselves the Churchill Club, so named because Winston Churchill was Knud's hero for spearheading the valiant war against the Nazis.

They had the perfect headquarters for their clandestine resistance group: the labyrinthine medieval Holy Ghost Monastery, which was the Pedersen family home, as well as housing the Reverend Edvard Pedersen's *Danske Folkekirke*, or Danish People's Church. Knud and Jens had bedrooms on a top floor, secluded from the rest of the family. The club would convene in Jen's bedroom, because he was a neat and tidy youth and there was room to sit down. There wasn't an inch of free space in Knud's room; a budding artist, he had crammed it with stacks of canvases and murky jars of paintbrushes and the floor was strewn with drawings and sketchbooks.

Things kicked off shortly before Christmas 1941. Knud, Jens and four classmates – Eigil Astrup-Frederiksen, Helge Milo, Mogens Thomsen and Mogens Fjellerup – were sitting around, smoking their pipes (pipe-smoking was the fad at the time amongst these academic Danish teenagers) and bristling with anger over the humiliation of living under Nazi occupation. There were German soldiers everywhere in Aalborg, smugly sauntering around, often arm in arm with their new Danish girlfriends, scoffing pastries at the smartest cafés. If you accidentally knocked into one on the street you were supposed to lower your gaze, doff your hat and apologise profusely. There was good reason for the heavy German presence in Aalborg: its airport was a strategically vital transportation hub and refuelling stop for the Wehrmacht en route to Norway and the ice-free harbours Hitler was intent on securing at all costs, in order to control the North Atlantic.

The boys had heard about the slaughter of Norwegian soldiers and citizens who resisted the Nazis. The two Scandinavian peoples were culturally very close and these occurrences sickened them. How could their fellow Danes not rise up in protest? Instead they were doing lucrative business with the Germans, selling them goods and even turning over some factories to produce materiel for the German military. Not for nothing did Churchill describe Denmark in the early years of the war as 'Hitler's tame canary'.

From the start of the occupation, Denmark – designated a 'protectorate' of Germany as opposed to conquered territory – had been promised political independence if the government allowed the German military to operate freely, and to ensure that there would be no resistance. And so far there hadn't been. But no one had reckoned on the Churchill Club.

So, back to that December evening in Jens's bedroom. The members of the newly formed club had begun to organise themselves into a proper resistance unit when there was an unexpected knock on the heavy wooden door. Knud opened it a crack to find a diminutive blond boy with blue eyes and an innocent face – it was Børge Ollendorff, the younger brother of Jens's school friend, Preben. He had heard about the club from his brother and was keen to join. Although only 14, Børge had brought a handy calling card: a tobacco pouch stuffed with the finest product from his father's tobacco company, and the promise of a regular supply. He was in.

The club was divided into three sections – propaganda, technical and sabotage. The propaganda section would paint anti-Nazi messages on buildings all around the city, sending a clear signal that not everyone in Aalborg was taking the occupation lying down. The technical section would make bombs and explosives in order to destroy specially chosen German targets. (This would be Mogens Fjellerup's area; as the school's top physics pupil he had been nicknamed 'the Professor'. The school even gave him his own key to the physics lab, allowing access to all manner of explosive chemicals.) Lastly there was the sabotage section, those intrepid members whose task would be to venture out and blow things up.

The rules were that no adult must know about the club, nor should it be mentioned to any outsider, and that in order to remain in the club each member had to commit a major anti-German act such as stealing a soldier's weapon, so that they were all equally culpable. They would meet after school and carry out their strikes in daylight, making quick getaways by bicycle. But if they needed to perform an act of sabotage at night they would tell their parents they were out playing bridge – at the home of their only friend without a telephone.

Over the following weeks in early 1942 they got stuck in, sowing confusion on the road network by destroying or repositioning road signs, sending truckloads of German troops rumbling off in the wrong direction. They cut German military telephone wires. And with bright blue paint they scrawled the word *vaernemager*, meaning 'war profiteer', on the premises of Nazi-sympathising businessmen. They also devised their own insignia – a mocking version of the swastika, with arrows pointing in all directions – and painted it on German army vehicles and barrack walls.

The boys knew that none of this would defeat the Nazis but they were useful exercises, getting them accustomed to being around danger, to taking risks. They had to learn to 'breathe normally' around armed German soldiers and not seize up with fear, so that they would be able to handle the greater hazards to come.

By February they were ready to make a bigger strike. The Fuchs Construction Company was based at Aalborg airport and built runways, hangars and other buildings for the Germany military. It represented everything the Churchill Club boys hated about the Danes' willing contribution to the Nazi war effort. They decided to set fire to it.

Knud and three of the others cycled off after dark into the city's outskirts, along snow-covered deserted roads, and when they neared the airport they abandoned their bikes and cut a hole through the wire perimeter fence. They crept up to the darkened Fuchs building, broke a window and climbed through into an office full of desks with architectural drawings and blueprints, bills, letters and other business documents. They put them all into a big pile, smashed a framed picture of Hitler on top of it and set it ablaze. Then they hightailed it back to their bikes and pedalled off for home, as the fire's orange glow appeared in windows behind them.

The building didn't burn down but with the company's plans and blueprints destroyed, the architects were forced to start over again.

Next they launched a series of lightning strikes against German army vehicles: anything from nifty little roadsters to lumbering trucks. A pair of boys would creep up to a vehicle, look inside to make sure no one was in it, then pour petrol on to the seats and toss in a lighted match. In seconds it would be in flames. At other times they would merely disable a vehicle by prising off the radiator grill and destroying the exposed parts, before painting their by now familiar insignia on it: they had created a form of 'branded resistance'.

Inevitably perhaps, the boys began to steal firearms. Not that they knew how to use them. But as a serious, organised underground movement, they felt it only right to have a stash of weapons, so that when the Allies came to liberate Denmark – as they inevitably would one day – they would be ready and able to join the fight.

They thought up cunning ways to relieve German soldiers of their weapons. Once Knud and Børge saw a lone soldier guarding a line of roadsters behind a fence and noticed a pistol lying on the seat of the nearest one. Some kids were playing football in the street and at one point their ball rolled towards Børge, who swiftly kicked it over the fence. It ended up under one of the roadsters. Knud approached the soldier and asked to be allowed to fetch the ball. He agreed and opened the gate. While Børge distracted the German with an awkward bilingual conversation, Knud retrieved the ball, and on his way out he reached into the end roadster, grabbed the pistol off the seat and hid it on his person. Then he gave the kids back their football and he and Børge calmly strolled away.

On another occasion, Knud was cycling around on 'routine reconnaissance' when, riding slowly alongside a German barracks, he looked through an open window and saw a rifle hanging from a bedpost. He had to have it! He quickly cycled off to gather the other club members for an urgent meeting back at their monastery HQ. They needed to work out a plan.

Before long they were all holed up in Jens's room at the top of the creaking old edifice, smoking their pipes and devising a scheme. There were now eight active Churchill Club members, including newcomer Uffe Darket, a friend from another school whose polite and respectable persona was the perfect disguise for a secret saboteur. (The Reverend Pedersen and his wife were delighted that their sons had such a fine group of friends, well-mannered boys with whom they had intelligent discussions and played bridge …) They sat in a swirl of pipe smoke, courtesy of Børge's father's tobacco, and decided that the rifle-nabbing operation would require three of them. One to nab the coveted prize, the other two to conceal it in a raincoat and transport it back to base.

An hour later Knud, Børge and Mogens Thomsen cycled to the barracks. Happily the rifle was still there, hanging from the bedpost. Knud slipped through a gap in the loose barbed wire fence. But as he approached the open window, to his alarm he saw a German soldier busily cleaning another window in the next room. He was facing the other way, thankfully — otherwise the game would have been over — but he was heart-stoppingly close.

Doing his best to calm his nerves, Knud reached in and carefully unhooked the rifle. He stepped away quickly and passed it through the fence to Børge, who in turn handed it to Mogens. It was wrapped in the raincoat and then put on to Mogens' bike. Then the three made their way back to the monastery, using quiet side roads, but with frequent stops to adjust the raincoat as the rifle kept poking out at both ends.

Another clever ruse they employed was to enter restaurants and cafés frequented by Wehrmacht officers and, when no one was looking, duck into the cloakroom – a place which could offer up real gems. Often, along with their coats and caps, the officers checked in their holstered sidearms. (A sign of how secure they felt in the 'tame' Scandinavian country they had occupied.) A quick riffle through a cloakroom's hanging garments had occasionally proved rewarding for a Churchill Club boy. If he was seen and questioned, he could always claim he was looking for a misplaced coat.

Gradually during the spring they collected an arsenal of pistols, rifles, grenades, knives, bayonets, ammunition, and even a machine gun which had been left unattended by two particularly careless members of the 'Master Race'. They had found a convenient hiding place for this hoard in the spooky vaulted basement of the ancient monastery.

But now they had to learn to shoot. And fortunately the monastery provided a suitable location for that, too: the enormous loft. Target practice took place during the reverend's church services, when the swelling organ music drowned out the sound of rifle shots and machine-gun fire. The boys lay on their stomachs at one end of the loft and aimed at targets attached to bales of hay at the other. Their aim wasn't always very good and sometimes they discharged their weapons by accident and nearly shot each other. Eigil once put a bullet through his own trousers, fortunately missing his legs.

So far the Churchill Club boys had been getting away with their repeated strikes against the occupiers – the theft and destruction of German property, the anti-Nazi graffiti liberally painted on walls – but each action further outraged the German authorities and now they gave the Danish police an ultimatum: either they track down and arrest the perpetrators, or the Gestapo would be brought in to do the job for them. Eigil's older sister, who worked as a secretary for the Aalborg police, was the only person outside the club to know about it and acted as its mole. She had disturbing news for its members: a pair of top detectives had been sent from Copenhagen to investigate the case. Apparently, the boys had been noticed during some of their thefts of weapons and witnesses were coming forward; the net was closing in. She begged them to stop their resistance.

But they had no intention of doing that. On the contrary. They were presented with an opportunity for their boldest attack yet, thanks to that image of propriety, Uffe Darket. At meetings of his model-aeroplane-building group Uffe had got to know three fellow hobbyists – factory workers in their early twenties – and sensing that he could trust them, told them about the Churchill Club. It turned out that they were just as keen on sabotage as the younger activists, and had recently stolen six mortar grenades from a railway station. Having no idea how to use them, they offered them to Uffe and his mates.

Jens smuggled the metal grenades, shaped like bowling pins, into the monastery and the boys tinkered with them, trying to figure out how they worked. Mogens the Professor inadvertently set one on fire, to general panic and much rushing about with buckets of water, before discovering that the grenades contained a flammable magnesium disc which could be lit with a match and serve as a firebomb.

And so to the big mission. They decided to stage an attack at the Aalborg railway yard. It was under constant use by the Nazis and awash with loaded freight trains containing valuable iron ore, machine parts and other vital supplies for the German military. The aim was to ignite a couple of these boxcars with the grenades. On the night of 2 May 1942, five of the boys cycled to the noisy, floodlit railway yard. They evaded the armed guards patrolling the perimeter fence, cut a hole through it and took up positions near the freight trains. Three of them acted as lookouts, armed with pistols which (mercifully) they had no reason to use.

Knud opened the door to one of the boxcars and saw to his delight that it was packed with aeroplane wings for the Luftwaffe, along with printed assembly instructions – a high-value target. The detested Luftwaffe had spent eight months mercilessly pounding British cities during the Blitz. Destroying the wings would be a small but attention-grabbing act of revenge. He put his grenade disc on to the pile of papers and aeroplane wings and threw in his match. The explosion was almost instant. One of the other boys did the same thing at the next boxcar along, and they fled the scene unimpeded. A triumph!

But their jubilation was short-lived. By now the ace investigators from Copenhagen had zeroed in on the Cathedral School as the heart of the Aalborg resistance. Knud in particular had been identified as a boy suspected of filching German officers' pistols from the cloakroom of Café Holle, by a waitress working there. As he and Helge left school together on the afternoon of 6 May, the police picked them up. Within hours, all eight members of the Churchill Club had been arrested and the police station was full of shocked and horrified parents – respectable professional people and wealthy business-owners, the city's elite – who had just learned that their privileged offspring were admitting guilt to some very serious crimes. Realising the game was up, Jens had led police to the weapons stash in the basement.

It wasn't looking good for the Aalborg Eight.

Needless to say, the Nazis were itching to punish the schoolboy saboteurs who had caused such destruction and cost them so much money. But they were Danes and their crimes had taken place on Danish soil. As a protectorate nation, Denmark was still in charge of its own legal and judicial system, so it claimed the right to try them in a Danish court. The Germans argued for trial in a German military court.

This was no small matter. With a German-led trial they would, at best, be sent to a concentration camp where survival was doubtful. At worst they would be executed, as saboteurs and resisters had been elsewhere under Nazi occupation. The Danes, in accordance with their very different laws, would punish them with relatively short sentences in a Danish prison.

In the end the Danes' will prevailed. But the Germans insisted on a proviso: they would appoint an official to be present throughout the trial to monitor proceedings and report back to Berlin.

At 14, Børge was too young for prison, so he was dispatched to a juvenile correctional institution. The remaining seven were put into Aalborg's King Hans Gades Gaol to await trial, and as it would be Denmark's first trial of anti-Nazi resisters, it was awaited with no small degree of public interest.

As well as harsh critics, the boys had many sympathisers amongst the population. After all, weren't they just a bunch of adventurous lads, standing up for their country? Aalborg's best cafés had pastries and cream cakes delivered to their cells.

Orderly Jens and shambolic Knud had been put into a small cell together – a recipe for disaster. Their growing tensions eventually erupted in an ugly brawl and the brothers were separated.

But by far the bigger problem arose during the trial a few weeks later, when Knud ignored his defence lawyer's instructions to show contrition for his actions and to claim that he had stolen weapons only to have them as souvenirs – a boy's wartime keepsakes – and not to use against anyone. Instead, when his turn came to speak, the 16-year-old told the court frankly that his intention had been to support the British in the forthcoming fight to liberate Denmark, and his only regret was that he and the others had been caught.

The seven boys were found guilty of wanton destruction of property, arson and theft of weapons from the German military. As the perceived leaders of their 'gang', Knud and Jens were sentenced to three years each; the others got lesser spells of eighteen months to two-and-a-half years. Under Danish law they could be released after serving two-thirds of their sentences.

In due course they were transferred to Nyborg State Prison, some 200 miles away – not quite as cosy as the local gaol and there were no pastry deliveries, but a far cry from Dachau.

The Churchill Club boys and their derring-do in the name of Danish independence were, at least covertly, applauded by a growing number of their fellow countrymen. They were given credit for rousing the nation's conscience. The year after their arrest, the RAF dropped leaflets over Denmark relating the story of the Churchill Club and lauding the actions of the 'schoolboys of Aalborg'. And they were inspiring other groups of schoolboys who were, in turn, caught by the police.

Throughout 1943 the Danes' hostility towards their occupiers increased and there were widespread strikes amongst Danish workers. At the end of August, the government refused to comply with draconian demands for a ban on strikes and public assembly, the introduction of a curfew and the death penalty for saboteurs. As a result, a day later the Germans dissolved the Danish government, declared martial law and subjected Denmark to the full severities of occupational rule.

The following month, a group of resistance movements joined together to form the Danish Freedom Council. And in the end the Danish Resistance, which had been so slow to get going, became one of the most celebrated underground organisations of the Second World War. In October 1943 it secretly evacuated almost all the country's 7,800 Jews by sea to neutral Sweden before the Nazis had a chance to murder them: a unique feat.

Chapter Ten

And not Forgetting Masha Bruskina, Bernard Bouveret and Helmuth Hübener

Masha was a middle-class Jewish girl who escaped from the Minsk ghetto in Belorussia, where she had been living with her mother, a manager with the state publishing company. Lightening her dark brown hair and adopting her mother's Aryan-sounding name of Anya, she remained in the city under the false identity of a Russian gentile and got a job as a medical assistant in a prison hospital at which the Nazis held wounded Soviet PoWs. She also joined a communist resistance cell which was making plans to liberate fifteen of the hospital's wounded Soviet army officers.

Masha was responsible for smuggling in civilian clothes and false documents to be used by the escaping officers, a task she completed with confidence. By mid-October 1941 the plan was ready to be set in motion. The Soviet army major in charge of leading the escape attempt warned Masha to leave Minsk before it was too late, but she refused to go.

The escapees managed to slip out of the hospital and escape from the city, but two days later they were captured by a German army patrol and all were summarily executed, except for a lieutenant who allegedly saved his life by giving up the names of the Resistance members who had helped them. According to another account, Masha's secret activities had already been observed by an unnamed person at the hospital, who betrayed her. Either way, the Gestapo soon had Masha under arrest, along with two others in her underground cell.

Despite the beatings and torture she suffered, Masha revealed nothing to her captors. She even managed to retain a dark sense of humour, remarking to a fellow prisoner, 'In any case, there's no chance I'll die of starvation.'

On 20 October she wrote a letter to her mother:

> I am tormented by the thought that I have caused you great
> worry. Don't worry. Nothing bad has happened to me. I swear
> to you that you will have no further unpleasantness because of
> me. If you can, please send me my dress, my green blouse and
> white socks. I want to be dressed decently when I leave here.

She already knew that she would be departing the prison only for her
execution, but didn't want to go to her death in dirty and bloodied
clothes.

The Germans decided to make an example of Masha and the
others with a highly visible public hanging. On Sunday, 26 October
1941, she was paraded through the streets flanked by her fellow
Resistance members, 16-year-old Volodya Sherbateyvich and a middle-
aged First World War veteran called Kiril Trus. Their hands were
tied behind their backs and a placard had been placed around
Masha's neck which read – in both German and Russian – 'We
are partisans and have shot at German troops', a blatant falsehood.
Masha, aged 17, walked calmly and with poise in her simple dress
and light-coloured cardigan, looking straight ahead.

The three were led to a small courtyard in front of the Minsk
Kristall yeast brewery and distillery plant. Masha was first to be taken
to the makeshift gallows. A stool was brought out from the factory
and Masha was made to stand on it. A crowd had gathered and her
executioners wanted her to face it, in order to suffer the full public
degradation, but she turned away towards a wooden fence at the side.
No matter how much they pushed her and tried to turn her around,
she resolutely remained with her back to the crowd. Finally they just
kicked the stool away. The entire event was recorded in a series of
photographs by a Lithuanian Nazi collaborator and to make sure the
message got through, the Germans left the bodies hanging for three
days before allowing them to be cut down and buried. Masha is widely
believed to have been the first person publicly executed during the
Nazi occupation of Soviet territory, which began only four months
earlier, in June, with Operation Barbarossa.

After the war, the shocking photographs of the execution of Masha, Volodya and Kiril were widely circulated. But while the Soviet authorities named the other two and officially recognised them as Soviet patriots and heroes of the Resistance, Masha was described simply as the 'unknown girl'. Decades after her identity had become well known, the authorities continued to deny knowledge of it, apparently due to Soviet anti-Semitism. It wasn't until 2009 that the municipality of Minsk, in modern-day Belarus, finally amended the monument at the execution site and replaced the words 'unknown girl' with Masha's full name.

In Israel too, she is remembered. There is a street named after her in Jerusalem.

Bernard Bouveret

French youth Bernard was recruited by a family friend, the watchmaker and Swiss spy Fred Reymond, into the Swiss secret service in 1941. He was 16 and living in the village of Chapelle-des-Bois in Vallée de Joux, a valley of the Jura Mountains, where his family had a restaurant and bakery. His village was conveniently located on the edge of the huge Risoux forest which straddled the French-Swiss border, and within a year or so of joining Fred's small band of covert operatives Bernard was smuggling Jews, resistance fighters, British airmen and those evading forced labour in the Reich, from occupied France into Switzerland. He also passed on information about German troop movements in and around his village, and carried clandestine messages and microfilm hidden in containers of aspirin, destined for Swiss intelligence and the British embassy in Berne. In the opposite direction, he smuggled hand grenades and explosives for the Maquis.

Bernard relished this opportunity to defy the Nazis. And he had the perfect cover story. As a wood-cutter whose daily work took him into the dense forest, he had every reason to be there. German soldiers would see him toiling amongst the trees in the daytime, check his papers and let him carry on. But once or twice a week after dark – under the noses of the Germans garrisoned barely 100 metres from his house –

he would cross the waist-high stone boundary wall which marked the border with Switzerland. With him would be the escapees whose lives were in his hands: sometimes a lone person or a couple, at other times a whole family of perhaps a dozen members. Often he would carry a small child on his shoulders. On one particularly alarming occasion, the father of a family group suffered an epileptic seizure while on the most dangerous stretch of their route. No one spoke on these smuggling missions; everyone was scared and it was better if Bernard didn't know the escapees' names or anything about them.

Once over the border, the group would rest and recover from the arduous journey at one of two wooden huts in the forest: the *Hôtel d'Italie* or the *Rendezvous des Sages*. From there they would be picked up by Fred Reymond or one of his operatives, who would guide them the rest of the way – several more kilometres – until they exited the forest. Meanwhile Bernard made his way back to Chapelle-des-Bois, creeping unseen into his house in the early hours of the morning.

These journeys were especially tough in the freezing winter. Some-times Bernard and his group had to travel on skis through the heavy snow, careful to avoid injury on the narrow trails between the trees and the rocks. And because footsteps and ski tracks in the snow would be a dead giveaway to German pursuers, Bernard and the other smugglers spent a lot of time making false tracks which looped around, leading nowhere, so that in the end the Germans gave up following them. But regardless of the season, these escapes were always a highly risky endeavour. The forest was patrolled, there was a curfew in operation between 11pm and 5am and anyone caught there during those hours was shot on sight. In order to evade the night patrols, Bernard and his fellow smugglers – known as *passeurs* – relied on their knowledge of the complex maze of trails, mostly unused by the Germans. Some *passeurs* were nevertheless captured or killed. One of Bernard's friends, aged 19, was shot with an explosive bullet in the middle of the night and perished in the snow.

Even after they had made it into Switzerland, the problems weren't over. Swiss customs officials had orders to arrest any fugitives picked up at the border and send them back to France. According to the law, refugees had to reach at least 10 kilometres inside Swiss territory before they could register to stay for the remainder of the war in an internment camp for illegal foreigners. The *passeurs* were only the first link in a wider network of Swiss and Free French intelligence agents, underground members and ordinary civilians involved in the rescues. After being delivered across the Swiss border, escapees were hidden with sympathisers before boarding trains that took them deeper into the country, from where they could seek asylum. Fred Reymond and his wife, whose house was near the border, personally sheltered, fed and bought train tickets for many of the fugitives. By the end of the war, many hundreds had been saved via the *passeurs*' Risoux forest escape route.

Bernard's covert activities came to an abrupt end in April 1944, when the Gestapo finally caught up with him. His father Jules – himself a *passeur* – was also arrested after his wife, Bernard's stepmother, was tricked by a French collaborator into giving him away. Fortunately for Bernard, his stepmother was unaware that he too had been working for a member of the Swiss secret service. She knew only that he made illegal trips to Switzerland, from where he brought her back gifts of contraband coffee, chocolate, pasta or cigarettes. But that was incriminating enough for the suspicious Gestapo. After their interrogation, both father and son were dispatched to Dachau concentration camp. There they remained for nearly a year, until liberated by American troops.

For years after the war the Swiss government viewed what the *passeurs* had done as civil disobedience. They were accused of pro-fiteering by selling contraband and charging money for smuggling people to freedom. In fact, Bernard was rarely given money for what he did. Nevertheless many *passeurs* were ostracised and fined, some were even imprisoned. But in 2009 a federal commission reversed that judgement, ruled that they had been wrongly penalised, and at long last recognised the bravery and self-sacrifice of Fred Reymond and his *passeurs*.

In 2014, a memorial honouring the wartime Risoux forest smugglers was unveiled in the Swiss hamlet of Abbaye by the Vallée de Joux authorities. Bernard Bouveret, by now a highly respected recipient of the *Légion d'Honneur*, was in attendance, the last one still alive. When speaking about his wartime exploits, which he occasionally does for groups of French schoolchildren, the nonagenarian admits that they still cause him occasional nightmares.

Helmuth Hübener

The Hübener family lived in the northern German city of Hamburg and belonged to the Church of Jesus Christ of Latter-day Saints (the Mormons). As a 10-year-old in 1935, the sporty and adventurous Helmuth joined the *Deutsches Jungvolk*, junior branch of the Hitler Youth. But his taste for it ended three years later with Kristallnacht, when he witnessed the wanton destruction of Jewish businesses and homes, in which the Hitler Youth eagerly took part.

At 16 he left school and started working at the Hamburg *Sozial-behörde*, the social welfare authority. It was 1941, two years into the war, and his loathing of Hitler and the Nazi regime had been growing steadily. He no longer trusted any news of the war churned out by Joseph Goebbels' propaganda machine on the officially approved radio stations. Then one day he came across a small Rola shortwave radio which had been left behind by his older half-brother Gerhard, a soldier in the Wehrmacht, while home on leave. That night Helmuth fiddled with the dial until he found the crackly German-language broadcast from the BBC in London. It changed everything. Finally an information source he instinctively felt he could trust. And its news of the war's progress contradicted reports put out by the German government.

Helmuth knew that listening to enemy broadcasts – known as *schwartzhören*, black listening – was strictly forbidden, being considered a form of treason. He couldn't do it at home. As his mother was out working and he didn't get along with his Nazi-sympathising stepfather, it made sense for him to move in with his maternal grandparents, who lived nearby. The elderly couple lived a quiet life and went to bed early, leaving him free to switch on the little radio each night and stay up late listening to the BBC.

He soon shared this secret activity with his two closest friends, Karl-Heinz Schnibbe, who was 17, and Rudolf (Rudi) Wobbe, 15, fellow members of his Mormon congregation. Wary of getting too involved, Karl-Heinz and Rudi were nonetheless intrigued by the revelations. But Helmuth didn't stop there. He had a grand plan. He would take the information he heard and write about it in flyers and leaflets to be distributed to the citizens of Hamburg. He wanted to make them *think*. If only they knew the truth, he reckoned, they would stop supporting Hitler's immoral regime. With a typewriter given to him by his church, for which he carried out informal secretarial duties, and paper taken from the office where he worked, he had the tools he needed. Late into the night he typed his anti-Nazi tracts and gave them headings such as 'Hitler the Murderer', 'Hitler the People's Seducer' and 'Hitler – the Guilty One'. He told his readers that contrary to Nazi propaganda, America's ability to fight a war had not been destroyed by the attack on Pearl Harbor. And that the fighting on the Eastern Front wasn't going as well as the German government claimed. He also railed against the 'criminal behaviour' of Hitler's top henchmen and the systematic persecution of the Jews. The war was futile, he wrote, and Germany was fated to lose it.

Helmuth composed dozens of leaflets on his typewriter, pounding the keys hard in order to make up to eight carbon copies at a time, and enlisted Karl-Heinz and Rudi to help distribute them around Hamburg after dark. Surreptitiously, nerves jangling, they pinned them on public bulletin boards, dropped them through letterboxes and placed them in phone booths.

On the Sunday following the first of these distribution exercises, as they were gathering in church for their Mormon service, Helmuth spotted Karl-Heinz sitting in the congregation a few rows ahead. 'So they haven't arrested you yet?' he shouted to his friend, laughing. Karl-Heinz, mortified, pleaded with him to shut up.

Of the hundreds of leaflets distributed, only a handful were handed in by disapproving citizens to the Gestapo, who assumed from the sophistication of the writing that the author was someone much older, perhaps a teacher or even a university professor.

In February 1942, Helmuth made the fatal error of showing one of his leaflets to a French-speaking work colleague, with the intention of asking him to translate it for the benefit of French PoWs. Instead he was denounced, and the very same day the Gestapo arrived at their office to arrest him. They took him to his grandparents' apartment, where they found the illegal radio and the typewriter with an unfinished leaflet still in it.

Under torture he revealed the names of his two friends, as the only other people who knew about the leaflets – but insisted they had been uninvolved in their distribution. Karl-Heinz and Rudi were quickly arrested in turn. But it took weeks of further vicious treatment of the boys before their interrogators were satisfied that Helmuth had acted entirely of his own accord and there had been no adult – conceivably a Mormon Church leader – orchestrating his subversive actions.

In August, the three were tried in Berlin at the *Volksgerichtshof*, the Special People's Court whose rabidly pro-Nazi judges had been personally appointed by Hitler. The merciless nature of the verdicts it handed down had earned it the epithet of Blood Tribunal.

One of the judges eyed Helmuth sternly and asked him: 'Young man, do you honestly believe that Germany will lose the war?'

Helmuth coolly replied: 'Don't you?'

The outraged judges murmured amongst themselves. 'Are you saying our German radio broadcasts are wrong and the English ones are accurate?' asked another.

'Exactly.'

Helmuth realised his life was over. He had nothing more to lose.

The verdicts were read out. Karl-Heinz and Rudi were sentenced to long terms in a hard-labour prison camp. Helmuth was sentenced to death for treason.

The boys were asked whether they had anything to say. The other two declined but Helmuth said yes. He stood and faced the judges. 'I have to die for no crime at all,' he declared, fixing them with a steady gaze. 'But your turn is next.'

Some time later when the three boys parted, Helmuth to remain at Plötzensee Prison in Berlin, the others to be moved on, Karl-Heinz tried to comfort his friend: 'Surely they won't execute you. You'll see. There is an appeal, you'll be pardoned.' Helmuth was less optimistic. His large, dark blue eyes filling with tears, he answered simply: 'I hope you have a better life in a better Germany.' Then he cried and embraced his friends.

On 27 October he composed three farewell letters to family and friends, weeping as he wrote and smudging the ink with his tears. His strong religious faith helped him through the final hours; his conscience was clear. 'My father in Heaven knows that I have done nothing wrong,' he wrote. 'I know that God lives and He will be the proper judge of this matter.' That evening he was guillotined at Plötzensee Prison. Of the nearly 3,000 prisoners executed there during the Nazi era, 17-year-old Helmuth was the youngest.

For many years after the war, Helmuth and his bold anti-Nazi campaign were forgotten. But in the 1960s he was rediscovered by a young German journalist, Ulrich Sander, whose numerous articles about the 'Helmuth Hübener group' raised public awareness of the three boys and eventually they were officially recognised as resistance fighters against the Third Reich.

The Mormon Church, which during the war disassociated itself from Helmuth so as not to jeopardise its existence in Nazi Germany (it was only faintly tolerated as an 'American institution'), later honoured him as a Mormon martyr to the truth of his political convictions.

In Hamburg and Berlin today there are memorials commemorating Helmuth Hübener. Streets, buildings, schools and youth centres have been named after him. The names of his judges on the Blood Tribunal, on the other hand, have been obscured by history.

In the early 1950s, both Karl-Heinz Schnibbe and Rudi Wobbe emigrated to America. Still faithful members of the Mormon Church, they settled in Salt Lake City, Utah, its world headquarters. In 1985 they were invited by the West German government to a ceremony honouring them as wartime resisters.

Rudi died of cancer aged 65 in 1992. Karl-Heinz lived on, often talking to students and other organisations about his wartime experiences, until he too passed away in 2010.

Epilogue

Stefania and Helena Podgorska

After the war Stefania – Fusia – married the man who had first launched her into the life of a secret wartime rescuer, Max Diamant. He changed his name to Josef Burzminski and became a dentist. The couple emigrated to Israel in 1957 and in 1961 Josef was a witness at Adolf Eichmann's trial in Jerusalem. The following year the Burzminskis moved once again, to Boston in the United States, where Josef opened a dental surgery and they raised their son and daughter. Fusia's younger sister Helena remained in Poland, married and became a physician in the city of Wrocław.

In 1979, Yad Vashem, the World Holocaust Remembrance Centre in Jerusalem, named the Podgorska sisters Righteous Among Nations. Of the almost 27,000 people around the world who have been accorded this title, Helena was the youngest at the time of the actions for which she was honoured – an impressive distinction.

(War is full of ironies and one of the most striking is that Poland, arguably always amongst Europe's most anti-Semitic countries, is also the one with the greatest number by far of Yad Vashem's Righteous: nearly 7,000 Poles have been honoured for saving Jewish lives during the Holocaust. In a further irony, it seems clear that both the ingrained cultural anti-Semitism and in very many cases the profound dedication to saving lives, emanated from the same source: the influence of the Catholic Church.)

The Podgorska sisters' wartime story was told in a 1996 made-for-television feature film called Hidden in Silence, on which Stefania was a consultant. For many decades she struggled with her traumatic memories of the war, sobbing as she relived its events and suffering from insomnia. She seemed unable to escape its horrors and it wasn't until the last years of her life, when dementia had set in and the flashbacks stopped, that she was finally free of her demons and could laugh, sing and flirt with staff at her care home in Los Angeles, California. She died in 2018.

Helena is still in Poland, living a quiet and private life. Due to the continuing problem of anti-Semitism in that country, she chooses not to divulge her Holocaust rescue story to fellow Poles. As the sisters' own siblings disapproved of their rescue mission, contact with family members was severed in the years after the war.

Leibke Kaganowicz

Leibke changed his name to Leon Kahn after the war and in 1948 emigrated to Vancouver, Canada, in the guise of a tailor: one of the few occupations allowing entry into the country as a displaced person. As he knew nothing of tailoring it wasn't long before he had to find other ways of earning a living. Unusually for a Jew, he started a Christmas tree business. One day in 1957 a customer was so impressed by his flair for salesmanship that he offered Leon a job. The customer was Henry Block, partner in an emerging local real estate company called Block Brothers. Starting as a humble real estate agent, Leon eventually took over the construction wing of what became western Canada's largest real estate firm. In due course he left to establish his own successful property development company.

He married a fellow Holocaust survivor from their home town of Eisiskes, whom he met whilst on a visit to New York, and they went on to have four children. A philanthropist and pillar of Vancouver's Jewish community, Leon also devoted his time to giving talks about his wartime experiences at schools and Holocaust symposia. In 1978 he published his memoirs. He died in Vancouver in 2003, shortly after he and his wife Evelyn celebrated their fiftieth wedding anniversary.

Stephen Grady

At the war's end Stephen joined the British army and planned a military career but his father's early death put paid to that hope. He agreed to his mother's request that he return in Nieppe as head of the family and resume his work tending the war graves. For his part in the Resistance he received the *Croix de Guerre* from the French government and the Americans awarded him its highest civilian honour, the Medal of Freedom.

He eventually became director of all Commonwealth War Grave Commission cemeteries in France, before retiring in 1984 with an OBE. Afterwards he settled Greece, where he still lives. In recent years the octogenarian reflected: 'Nothing helps memories linger as much as fear, and I lived in terrible fear when I was growing up. Fear of being caught by the Germans, fear of being tortured by their police. Fear so intense I have never been able to obliterate it … I still sleep with a shotgun by the side of my bed. Just in case.'

He remained lifelong friends with his wartime buddy and ally Marcel Lombard, who has never moved far from Nieppe.

Truus and Freddie Oversteegen

With the advent of the Cold War in the late 1940s and early 1950s, Holland's erstwhile communist resistance fighters were out of favour with the Dutch government and not accorded formal recognition for their acts. Freddie married, had children and resigned herself to a quiet family life, although she found it impossible to shake off disturbing memories of the past. The nightmares never stopped, she acknowledged towards the end of her life.

Truus was more outspoken and had a more visible public life. She married a former comrade in the Resistance, had four children, and forged a career in Holland as a painter and sculptor. One of her most celebrated works is the bronze monument to Hannie Schaft in Haarlem's Kenaupark, unveiled by Queen Julianna in 1982.

'The tragedy of the war stayed with me all my life,' the elderly Truus admitted in an interview, 'but I paint and I sculpt and I am happy.' Asked about the multiple assassinations of Nazis and collaborators which she and her sister had carried out during the war she replied: 'We did not feel it suited us. [Killing] never suits anybody, unless they are real criminals. It poisons the beautiful things in life.'

Truus was named Righteous Among the Nations by Yad Vashem in 1967, and in 1998 was invested as an Officer of the Order of the Orange-Nassau. Then at last, in 2014 the Dutch government awarded the Oversteegen sisters the *Mobilisatie-Oorlogskruis* (War Mobilization Cross) in honour of their wartime resistance. Prime Minister Mark Rutte called the belated recognition 'an act of historical justice'.

Both women died at the age of 92, Truus in 2016 and Freddie in 2018.

Jacques Lusseyran

Jacques became a noted academic after the war. In 1958 he emigrated to America to teach French literature at the private Hollins University in Virginia. He remarked: 'I was born three times: when I came into the world, when I went blind, and when I boarded a ship for America.' While teaching at Hollins he often paced the stage of a lecture hall, a cigarette in his mouth. Students would hold their breath as he neared the edge, but he assured them they needn't worry as he was able to sense the objects around him. It was also said that he could identify each of his students by their footsteps as they entered his class, even if they wore different shoes.

He was later Associate Professor of Philosophy at Western Reserve University in Cleveland, Ohio, before becoming a professor at the University of Hawaii, and wrote philosophical essays. He never mentioned his wartime experiences to the many students he taught and it was only when his autobiography *And There Was Light* was published in the USA in 1963 that they learned what he had accomplished and what he had suffered. He was married three times and the father of four children. Tragically, he died together with his third wife Marie in a car accident in France in 1971, aged only 47.

Hortense Daman

When she returned to Leuven after the war, Hortense met an English soldier then stationed at the Philips factory across the square from the family home. He was Staff Sergeant Sydney Clews and the pair fell in love. They married the following year and settled in Newcastle-under-Lyme in Staffordshire. It was to be a while before Hortense learned the nature of the medical experiments carried out on her at Ravensbrück concentration camp. The near-fatal gangrene injection left her leg permanently impaired. But sixteen years after she had supposedly been sterilised by a camp doctor she gave birth to a daughter, and seven years later she had a son.

Hortense was widely lauded for her part in the Resistance. The Belgian government awarded her its Croix de Guerre and Medal of Resistance, she was appointed a Knight of the Order of Leopold II and she received the Partisan Medal from the Belgium Partisan Association. In England she was granted the freedom of the cities of London and Stoke-on-Trent, and for assisting in the rescue of Allied airmen she was elected an honorary member of the Aircrew Association. Her local borough council even named a housing complex after her.

She died in Newcastle-under-Lyme in 2006.

Adolfo Kaminsky

France awarded Adolfo the *Croix du Combattant*, *Croix du combattant volontaire de la Résistance* and the *Médaille de Vermeil de la ville de Paris* for his wartime acts. Afterwards in peacetime, far from giving up the forger's life, Adolfo spent almost another three decades churning out false documents for those he felt had a deserving cause. He provided false identity papers for Jews trying illegally to enter Palestine, as well as assisting the anti-British militants of the Irgun group. Later, as a fierce anti-imperialist, he became embroiled in Algeria's war of independence against France by forging documents for the National Liberation Front of Algeria and for French draft dodgers.

During the 1960s, he aided left-wing movements throughout Latin America – in Brazil, Argentina, Venezuela, El Salvador, Nicaragua, Colombia, Peru, Uruguay, Chile, Mexico and Haiti – as well as in Angola, South Africa, Portugal, Spain and Greece. He provided papers for American draft dodgers during the Vietnam War. Adolfo seemed markedly less interested, however, in helping dissidents in the repressive communist regimes of the period, such as the Soviet Union and its satellite states.

He never asked to be paid for his forgeries, instead earning his living through photography. In 1971, fearing his cover had been blown and the police were after him, he finally hung up his forger's tools and moved to Algiers, where he married a young native woman and had three children. He spent the next decade there but as Islamic fundamentalism tightened its hold on the country he was no longer safe as a Jew; his liberal-minded wife and half-Jewish children were equally at risk. So in 1982 they fled Algeria and sought refuge in France, eventually all becoming French citizens. No doubt the irony of fleeing a country whose liberation he had worked towards, for the safety of its former colonial ruler, did not escape the anti-imperialist. The nonagenarian still lives in Paris.

Edelweiss Pirates

Following the war, the Pirates were mostly viewed as petty criminals and misfits, rather than legitimate anti-Nazi resistance fighters. It didn't help their case that, mavericks to the end, they refused to get involved with the new officially sanctioned youth groups formed under Allied supervision. As for those unlucky enough to end up under Soviet control in what became East Germany, anyone proved to be a member of the Edelweiss Pirates received an automatic 25-year prison sentence.

As late as 1987 an investigation by the state of North Rhine-Westphalia decided to uphold the criminal records given to former Pirates by the Gestapo, despite the fact that three years earlier Yad Vashem had named three of them – Jean Jülich, Michael Jovy and Bartholomäus (Barthel) Schink – as Righteous Among the Nations for having risked their lives to save Jews.

In the new millennium the case was reopened by Cologne's District Governor, Jürgen Roters, with the aim of rehabilitating the Pirates and lifting the stigma surrounding them. The 2004 German feature film *Edelweisspiraten* helped to burnish their reputation as a band of bold anti-Nazi rebels and a year later the German government annulled their criminal records, officially recognising them as resistance fighters.

Jean Jülich – who ran a popular 'music pub' in Cologne after the war and initiated various cultural projects to promote post-war healing – was presented in 1991 with the *Bundesverdienstkreuz*, the Order of Merit of the Federal Republic of Germany, for his contribution to the process of reconciliation. And at last, in 2011 Fritz Theilen, Gertrud Koch and three other surviving Pirates received the same award, for their acts of anti-Nazi resistance decades earlier.

Jean died in 2011 and Fritz the following year. In 2016 the last of the Navajos, Gertrud – still going by her nickname 'Mucki' – died at the age of 92.

Today the Edelweiss Pirates are regarded as local folk heroes in Cologne, the city in which they operated most famously. The street beside the suburban railway station where the group of Pirates were hanged on that cold November morning in 1944 is now named Bartholomäus-Schink-Strasse. And at the city's annual *Edelweiß-piratenfestival*, attended by large crowds of enthusiasts, the defiant songs they once sang and strummed their guitars to fill the air again for new generations of young people.

The Churchill Club

Five years after the war, in the autumn of 1950, Winston Churchill visited Copenhagen in order to accept the Sonning Prize, a Danish award for outstanding contributions to European culture. On the flight from England he sat next to the Danish Resistance hero Ebbe Munck, who told him all about the exploits of the Churchill Club. 'Round up as many of them as possible,' said Churchill. 'I should like to acknowledge their contribution.' And so it was that at Copenhagen's 3,000-seat K.B. Hallen concert venue, Churchill greeted the former club members, now young men, who lined up before him; an event none of them could have imagined as they sat in prison cells a few years earlier.

Knud Pedersen became an artist and founded both a film school and a renowned art lending library in Copenhagen. He died in the city in 2014. His brother Jens, who became an engineer, died of lung cancer in 1988. A handful of the others are still alive. As for the venerable Holy Ghost Monastery – scene of wartime plotting, pipe-smoking and target practice – it has a more subdued role today, as a retirement home for the elderly.

Conclusion

During my months of research into the subject of youngsters involved in anti-Nazi activities, I was sometimes struck by the uncomfortable feeling that (hugely brave and admirable though they were), those boys and girls might have been better off staying out of trouble and waiting for the Allied armies and air forces to take their risks for them. After all, it was the Allies' combined military superiority which won the war, wasn't it? Did those countless acts of resistance – the sabotage, assassinations, underground newspapers – actually shorten the conflict at all, or help the Allies to win it?

Or would the war have played out much as it did over the course of its six years, even without them? Was all the torture and death at the hands of the SS and Gestapo, and all the hideous reprisals against randomly rounded-up innocents, a price worth paying for that resistance? This is an especially pertinent question as regards schoolchildren and juveniles whom no one would have blamed for staying out of the war. (The other form of resistance – i.e. rescuing Jews and other fugitives from the Nazis – was clearly in a different category, and a matter of the deadliest urgency. You couldn't wait for an Allied victory to save someone from Auschwitz.)

In raising these questions I was really hoping to hear, from a historian with specialist knowledge of the Second World War, that the sacrifices weren't for nothing. That the suffering and the lives lost – including those very young lives which feature in this book – did indeed make a significant contribution to the defeat of the Third Reich. So I turned to a friend, the historian Dr Helen Fry, to elicit her views. She has written extensively about the war, clandestine wartime operations and most pertinently about MI9, the War Office department tasked with supporting European resistance networks.

'These youngsters could easily have chosen a different path and remained bystanders,' she said. 'I think that is worth remembering. So why did they do it? I think their bravery was often partly driven by the belief that youth is invincible – that against the odds and the evidence around them, they would survive. (Of course the reality was very different.) Unmarked by the cares of middle age, these youngsters also saw resistance as a thrilling adventure. And youth is impatient. If they had waited for the Allied forces and not resisted, the outcome would have been different. They effected many small changes which rippled out – we mustn't underestimate the value that tiny acts of sabotage and resistance made in helping the Allies. The Allies needed to be able to work with the Underground and it was not uncommon for those even under 18 to help with both the Resistance and the escape lines; the Resistance worked cross-generationally. One wonders how the Nazi regime ever thought it could hold down a nation it was occupying; the spirit of resistance will win the day in the long run. The Germans had learnt nothing from their failure in the First World War.

'And don't forget, the parents of these children had fought the Germans just two decades years earlier in such a bloody war that no one was prepared to take chances in the second one. It was still fresh within the memories of parents and grandparents, and was passed down to the next generation.

'So we genuinely needed the resistance groups of all ages to prepare for when the Allies arrived – to have a network of "friends" in situ was essential. Even after the Allied forces crossed into occupied Europe, victory was not assured until about February 1945; the tide of the war could have turned. Hitler was still developing his secret weapons: by then it was the V3 "super gun".

'The ties between parts of Europe and Britain run very deep. We had to connect with underground resistance groups behind enemy lines, under the noses of the Germans – even though it was risky and came at a great cost to human life for the helpers. The youngsters were perfect, precisely because no one suspected them of being involved. In the end, each Resistance member, regardless of age, was essential in the chain.'

So in the final analysis, not only was the resistance essential, but it seems it couldn't have been any other way. Human nature dictated as much. Despite this, you can't help but wonder how you yourself would have felt had it been your own children endangering their lives to strike back at the Nazi oppressors. Would you have been proud of their courage and commitment to the cause, and with fearful heart accepted the risks? Or forbidden their involvement and done everything possible to get them out of harm's way? Ultimately, which is the greater impulse – a parent's instinct to preserve their child, or a citizen's hunger for justice and freedom? A matter for each person to mull over for himself, perhaps.

And with luck, we will never have to find out.

Sources

Books

Billstein, Reinhold; Fings, Karola; Kugler, Anita; Levis, Nicholas, *Working for the Enemy: Ford, General Motors, and Forced Labour in Germany during the Second World War* (Berghahn Books, New York, 2000)

Bles, Mark, *Child at War: The True Story of Hortense Daman* (Warner Books, London, 1992)

Bultman, Saskia (English language editor), *Yearbook of Women's History, Under Fire: Women and World War II* (Verloren Publishers, Hilversum, 2014)

Grady, Stephen, *Gardens of Stone: My Boyhood in the French Resistance*, with Michael Wright (Hodder & Stoughton, London, 2013)

Hoose, Phillip, *The Boys Who Challenged Hitler: Knud Pedersen and the Churchill Club* (Farrar, Straus & Giroux, New York, 2015)

Kahn, Leon, *No Time To Mourn*: *The True Story of a Jewish Partisan Fighter*, as told to Marjorie Morris (Ronsdale Press & Vancouver Holocaust Education Society, Vancouver, 2004)

Kaminsky, Sarah, *Adolfo Kaminsky: A Forger's Life*, English translation by Mike Mitchell (DoppelHouse Press, Los Angeles, 2016)

Lusseyran, Jacques, *And There was Light: The autobiography of a blind hero in the French resistance*, English translation by Elizabeth R. Cameron (Little, Brown and Company, Boston, 1963)

Menger, Truus, *Not Then, Not Now, Not Ever*, English translation by Rita Girour (Nederland Tolerant/Max Drukker Stichting, Haarlem, 1998)

Tuaillon-Nass, Gisele, *Le rendez-vous des sages*, (Presses du Belvedere, 2010)

Wagner, Meir, *The Righteous of Switzerland: Heroes of the Holocaust* (Ktav Publishing House Inc., Hoboken, 2001)

Feature Films

Edelweiss Pirates, Palladio Film, 2004
Hidden in Silence, Heart Entertainment Inc., 1996

Documentaries

Above and Beyond, WWII Foundation and Tim Gray Media, 2014
Corrie ten Boom: A Faith Undefeated, Herald Entertainment, Christian History Institute, 2013
Holocaust: Ravensbrück and Buchenwald, Chronos Productions, 2006
Making Choices: The Dutch Resistance During World War II, Robert Prince, University of Alaska Fairbanks, 2005
No. 4 Street of Our Lady, Barbara Bird, Judy Maltz and Richie Sherman, 2009
Portrait of a Soldier, Marianna Bukowksi, 2015
Secret Army: The Underground Auxiliary Units of WW2, Peter Williams, Meridian Broadcasting, 2003
The Forger, Manual Cinema Studios, 2016
The Hitler Youth: The Young People of the Third Reich, ZDF, 2000
Truth and Conviction: the Helmuth Hübener Story, BYU Broadcasting, 2002
Unlikely Heroes, Moriah Films, Film Division of the Simon Wiesenthal Centre, Los Angeles, California, 2003

Archives

Imperial War Museum oral history collection (1996 interview with Hortense Daman Clews)
Museum of Danish Resistance, Copenhagen
Museum of National Resistance, Champigny-sur-Marne
Noord-Hollands Archief, Haarlem
NS-Documentation Centre, Cologne
United States Holocaust Memorial Museum, Washington DC
USC Shoah Foundation, Institute for Visual History and Education, University of Southern California, Los Angeles

Vancouver Holocaust Education Centre
Verzets Resistance Museum, Amsterdam
Yad Vashem World Holocaust Remembrance Centre, Jerusalem

Newspapers and Websites

Blakemore, Erin, *Meet the Youngest Person Executed for Defying the Nazis*, (www.history.com, 27 October 2017)

Cazzola, Florian, *Bernard Bouveret, 92 ans, 'on passait des familles juives entières'* (www.francebleu.fr, 7 May 2017)

Childs, David, *Fritz Theilen: Member of the Edelweiss Pirates, the children who resisted Hitler* (The Independent, 3 May 2012)

Coles, John, *Truus Oversteegen – 16-year-old female Resistance fighter* (www.schoolofjandejong.blogspot.com, 28 February 2012)

Duerden, Nick, *My father's secret wartime exploits* (The Guardian, 16 March 2013)

Gersony, Marina, *Adolfo Kaminsky: Forger for the Good* (www.eastwest.eu, December 2011)

Hendler, Sefi, *Con Artist: The True Story of a Master Forger* (Haaretz, 7 March 2013)

Hochard, Cécile, *Le mouvement les Volontaires de la Liberté*, (www.museedelaresistanceenligne.org)

Hofman, Margie, *The Story of Michael Trotobas*, The Preservation Foundation, Inc (http://www.storyhouse.org, 1998)

Holocaust Life Stories, audiovisual collection of the Montreal Holocaust Museum, (www.holocaustlifestories.ca)

Jean Julich obituary (The Telegraph, 6 February 2012)

Johnson, Daniel, *Wartime 'people smugglers' finally feted as heroes* (www.swissinfo.ch, 8 October 2014)

Johnson, Pat, Vancouver's Unlikely Hero (Jewish Independent, 21 May 2004)

Joostens-Egret, Christine, *Bernard Bouveret, 92 ans, 'on passait des familles juives entières'* (www.francebleu.fr, 7 May 2017)

Keller, Bill, Echo of '41 in Minsk: Was the Heroine a Jew? (The New York Times, 15 September 1987)

Kellerman, Katie, *The Edelweiss Pirates: A Story of Freedom, Love and Life*, (International Raoul Wallenberg Foundation, www.raoul wallenberg.net, 6 August 2006)

Klein, Ansgar, S., Persoenlichkeiten/*jean-juelich* Portal Rheinische Geschichte (www.rheinische-geschichte.lvr.de, 9 April 2019)

Knowles, Tom, *Human spirit being 'overwhelmed by tech giants* (The Times, 25 April 2019)

Leafe, David, *Fighting the Germans at 17: The British boy who became the bravest man in the French Resistance* (Daily Mail, 19 February 2013)

Macey, Jennifer, *Campaigning for Cologne's Maligned Resistance* (www.dw.com, 10 November 2004)

Moriarty, Marilyn; Harris, Beth, *French Connections: Jacques Lusseyran at Hollins (Hollins Magazine, September 2018)*

Nuij, Norbert-Jan, Truus Oversteegen obituary www.resources.huygens.knaw.nl, 1 July 2017)

O'Leary, Naomi, *Her war never stopped: the Dutch teenager who resisted the Nazis* (The Guardian, 23 September 2018)

Olesen, Niels Wium, *Sleeping With the Enemy* (www.kulturarv.de)

Pliester, Jeroen, Truus Menger-Oversteegen obituary, National Hannie Schaft Foundation (www.hannieschaft.nl, 26 November 2016)

Reinhardt, Nora, *Fighting Nazis with Fakes: The Hidden Life of the Humanitarian Forger* (Spiegel Online, 25 August 2011)

Rosthorn, Andrew, *John Jülich: One of the Edelweiss Pirates, who resisted the Nazis* (The Independent, 10 November 2011)

Rowsell, Ali, *War Walks on the Swiss Jura Crest Trail*, www.cicerone. co.uk, 10 March 2019.

Smith, Harrison, Freddie Oversteegen obituary (*The Washington Post*, 17 September 2018)

Spanjer, Noor, *This 90-year-old Lady Seduced and Killed Nazis as a Teenager* (www.vice.com/en_uk, 11 May 2016)

Stories of Freedom: Hannie Schaft, (www.bevrijdingspop.nl, 24 February 2015)

Vast, Cécile, Philippe Viannay (www.museedelaresistanceenligne.org, 2004)

Index